2/27/03 fw

YOUR BRAIN HAS ASKED
ABOUT ITSELF BUT
COULDN'T ANSWER . . .
UNTIL NOW

101

QUESTIONS YOUR

BRAIN

HAS ASKED ABOUT ITSELF BUT COULDN'T ANSWER... UNTIL NOW

· · · · ·

FAITH HICKMAN BRYNIE

· · · · ·

THE MILLBROOK PRESS
BROOKFIELD, CONNECTICUT

Published by The Millbrook Press, Inc.
2 Old New Milford Road
Brookfield, CT   06804

Cover photograph courtesy of The Image Bank/© Peter Till
Photographs courtesy of Visuals Unlimited (© British Museum): p. 18;
Photo Researchers: pp. 28 James Holmes/SPL (both), 86 Science Photo
Library (left) Alfred Pasieka/SPL (center, right), 93 © 1984 Martin M.
Rotker (left) © Biophoto Associates/Science Source (right); © 1992 Rich
Saal: p. 45; © Marcus E. Raichle, M.D., Washington University School of
Medicine, St. Louis, Missouri: p. 47; H. Damasio, T. Grabowski, R. Frank,
A. M. Galaburda, A. R. Damasio: The return of Phineas Gage: Clues about
the brain from a famous patient. *Science*, 264:1102-1105, 1994.
Department of Neurology and Image Analysis Facility, University of Iowa: p.
82; UPI/Corbis-Bettmann: p. 89; Colorado State University: p. 99; Corbis-
Bettmann: p. 105; Corbis: p. 108. Illustrations by Sharon Lane Holm.

Library of Congress Cataloging-in-Publication Data
Brynie, Faith Hickman, 1946–
101 questions your brain has asked about itself but couldn't answer . . .
until now / by Faith Hickman Brynie.
p. cm.
Includes bibliographical references and index.
Summary: Provides information about the physical aspects of the brain
and how it functions, effects of diseases and drugs on the brain, memory,
senses, and more in question and answer format.
ISBN 0-7613-0400-2 (lib. bdg.)
1. Brain—Juvenile literature. 2. Neurophysiology—Juvenile literature.
3. Neurosciences—Juvenile literature. 4. Neuropsychology—Juvenile
literature. [1. Brain—Miscellanea. 2. Questions and answers.] I. Title.
QP361.5.B78 1998
612.8'2—dc2l   98-9797 CIP AC

CONTENTS

To those big brains
who made so much difference:
Kenneth Branch, Thelma Chedister,
Beatrice Law, and John Koburger.

The author gratefully acknowledges the expert critical reviews provided by Dr. Eric Chudler, University of Washington, and Dr. Marjorie Murray, Seattle, Washington. Thanks also to Dr. John Clark of Addenbrooke's Hospital, Cambridge, England, for his invaluable help with brain imaging technologies. And thanks to Mona Kunselman of the University of Washington's Making Connections Program for doing just that.

FOREWORD

The growth of the human mind is still high adventure,
in many ways the highest adventure on earth.

• NORMAN COUSINS •

What a marvelous organ—that brain of yours. First, it keeps you alive. From deep inside your brain radiate the messages that tell your heart to pump blood, your lungs to take in air, your kidneys to excrete wastes. Your brain makes you sleep, then wakes you. It tells you when you're thirsty or hungry. Pain interpreted by your brain lets you know when you're injured or sick.

In yet another of its roles, your brain makes your very survival possible. Taste spoiled food, and you'll spit it out. Fall in the dark, and you'll know how to right yourself. Smell smoke, and you'll run away from the fire. Even more impressive, your brain lets you make choices that may run counter to your instincts. Self-preservation says run away from that fire, but people have been known to rush into burning buildings to save someone they love.

It's no surprise that your brain makes you aware of your surroundings. But have you ever thought, at an even more basic level, that your brain is responsible for your sense that you are you? Your consciousness and your self-awareness are products of your brain. How? No one knows, just as no one knows how this incredible organ can do what no other organ can: it can study itself. That's what your brain decided to do the moment you opened this book.

On these pages, you'll find many questions and answers. Some may seem simple and obvious; others, complicated and difficult. All will make better sense if you keep two big ideas in mind:

- Different parts of the brain do different jobs.
- Much of the brain's work is done by chemicals called neurotransmitters. [Neurotransmitters are chemicals that carry (transmit) messages between nerve cells (neurons); hence the name neurotransmitters.]

Words such as acetylcholine or serotonin may sound difficult, but they are simply names for neurotransmitters. All are molecules that work because their shape fits a receptor site on a neuron, in much the same way that a key works because it fits a lock.

You may forget from one chapter to another what a brain area does, how a neurotransmitter operates, or what effect a drug has. That's to be expected from a healthy brain, and that's the reason for the tables at the back of the book. There's also a glossary to help you with the definitions of new or unfamiliar words. Use it whenever your memory needs a boost.

Speaking of memory, that's another of your brain's jobs, as you'll learn in Chapter Three. But let's begin at the beginning. . . .

CHAPTER ONE

THAT SHOULD COME FIRST

It is impossible to live without brains,
either one's own, or borrowed.

• BALTASAR GRACIAN •

What Is My Brain Anyway? That three pounds of mushy stuff inside your skull is the control center for everything you do, say, think, or know. It's made of about 100 billion nerve cells, or neurons, and the cells that support them, called glial cells.[1] That's as many cells as there are stars in the Milky Way.[2]

Some scientists say that humans have not one brain but three. The first—and the most primitive—is the brain stem. Sometimes called "the reptilian brain," the brain stem controls the body's basic functions such as breathing and heartbeat. At the rear of the brain stem lies the cerebellum, responsible for posture, movement, and physical skills.

The second brain is the limbic system or "old mammalian brain" common to all mammals. It comprises roughly one-fifth of the brain's

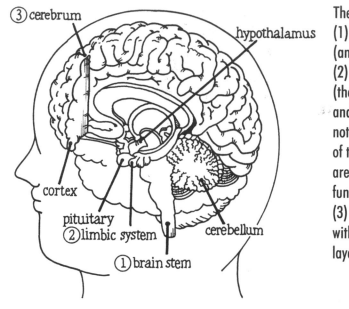

③ cerebrum

hypothalamus

cortex

pituitary
② limbic system

cerebellum

① brain stem

The three brains:
(1) the brain stem
(and cerebellum),
(2) the limbic system
(the hypothalamus
and pituitary, while
not technically part
of the limbic system,
are vital to its
function), and
(3) the cerebrum
with its thin outer
layer, the cortex.

area.[3] Along with the brain stem, it controls body temperature, blood pressure, heart rate, and blood sugar. It also governs emotions and behavior ranging from love to violence and aggression.

The third brain is the "new mammalian" or "thinking" brain—the cerebrum with its thin covering, the cortex. Here reside sensory perception, voluntary movement, conscious thought, purpose, personality—everything from smelling the roses to planning for the future.

When all is well, the three brains work in harmony. Connections between the brain stem and the limbic system help keep you conscious, alert, and in control. Communication between the limbic system and the cortex lets you balance logic and emotion, fact and feeling.

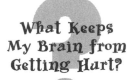

The bony shield that protects the brain is the skull. Just under the skull are three layers of protective tissue called the meninges. The cerebrospinal fluid inside is a floating support for both the brain and the spinal cord, the bundle of neurons encased by the backbone. The cord carries messages between the brain and the rest of the body.

Also, a network of cells in the blood vessels that supply the brain prevents some poisons from getting in. This network is called the blood-brain barrier.

The skull, backbone, meninges, and cerebrospinal fluid protect the brain and spinal cord.

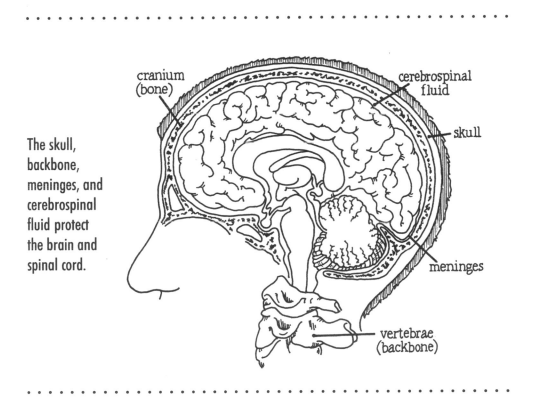

cranium (bone)

cerebrospinal fluid

skull

meninges

vertebrae (backbone)

Is a Headache Really a Brainache?

Poke it, tear it, or cut it, the brain has no feeling. It has no nerves that detect pain, even though it receives pain signals from other parts of the body. So what are headaches? Most are pain in the muscles of the face, neck, and head. You may think the headache you had last Friday came from worrying about a history test, but that's only indirectly true. What happened was that the strain of the test affected your posture. You hunched over your books, clenched your jaw, tightened your shoulders. The result? A tension headache.

Squinting because of poor vision may strain muscles in the forehead and cause a headache, as can eye diseases such as glaucoma and infections in the ear. Sometimes the culprit is a blockage or infection of the sinuses, air spaces connected with the nose that lie around the nose and behind the eyes and forehead.

The membranes that cover the surface of the brain can detect pain, and that's what hurts when a brain tumor or meningitis causes a headache. Another kind of headache comes from the swelling of blood vessels in the head, after consuming too much alcohol, for example.

Migraine headaches—those accompanied by visual disturbances or nausea—can be brought on by certain foods, menstruation, stress, or other factors. They may occur when blood vessels in the head first constrict and then expand, sending pain messages from all parts of the head to the brain. Some researchers blame migraines on the activation of a cell mass in the brain stem that can send pain signals.

What's the Largest Part of My Brain?

The cerebrum. That's the outermost, convoluted mass that you probably associate with the word brain. It has two halves: a left hemisphere and a right hemisphere, each controlling the opposite side of the body. The corpus callosum, a band of about 300 million nerve fibers,[4] connects the two hemispheres.

The cortex, a wrinkled layer less than one-quarter inch thick,[5] covers each hemisphere. More than seven of every ten neurons in the entire human nervous system are found in the cortex.[6] Because of your cortex you are able to organize, remember, communicate, understand, appreciate, and create.

The deeper parts of each hemisphere contain nerve fibers traveling to and from the cortex. Some of these clumps of neurons are associated with movement, others with emotions.

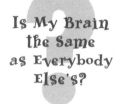

Is My Brain the Same as Everybody Else's?

Although people's brains don't look any different, they are as different as their faces. But— just as faces have similar parts such as eyes, nose, and mouth—our brains have similar recognizable parts, too. Everyone has four lobes in the cerebral cortex:

(1) the frontal under the forehead toward the top of the head

(2) the parietal at the crown of the head

(3) the occipital at the back of the head just above the cerebellum

(4) the temporal, along the side of the head behind the eyes and above the ears

Still, no two brains are exactly alike, a fact that poses some problems for scientists. Michael Gazzaniga, a famous brain scientist, says, "Every brain is different. . . . If we take our data and average them, we build an idealized brain that doesn't exist."[7]

What Different Jobs are Handled by Different Parts of My Cortex?

The frontal lobe is the largest of the four lobes of the cerebrum. That's where most planning, decision-making, and purposeful behavior begin. People with damaged frontal lobes can't adapt to new situations or understand complex ideas. The frontal lobe is well connected with the seat of emotions, the limbic system. Much of your awareness of danger comes from your frontal lobe as it processes signals from the brain's fear centers deep in the limbic system.

The parietal lobe is where your body processes the sensory information obtained from touch. It's also where letters form as words, and words combine into thoughts. Neurons there process information about the position of the body in space, muscles, touch, and pressure. The primary motor area just in front of the parietal lobe controls voluntary movement.

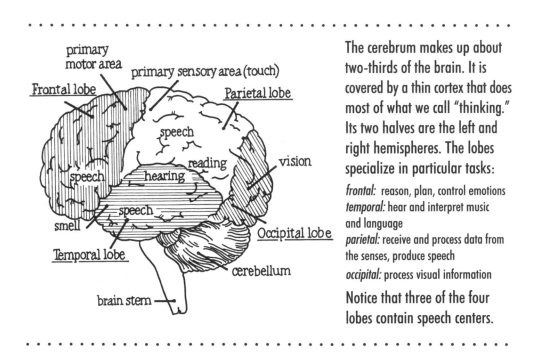

The cerebrum makes up about two-thirds of the brain. It is covered by a thin cortex that does most of what we call "thinking." Its two halves are the left and right hemispheres. The lobes specialize in particular tasks:

frontal: reason, plan, control emotions
temporal: hear and interpret music and language
parietal: receive and process data from the senses, produce speech
occipital: process visual information

Notice that three of the four lobes contain speech centers.

Because the occipital lobe handles vision, it is often called the visual cortex. Information goes from the eyes through a relay station to the visual cortex. Damage to the occipital lobes can result in blindness even if the rest of the visual system is normal.

The temporal lobe performs several functions, including hearing, perception, and some kinds of memory. An area of the temporal cortex about as big as a poker chip is responsible for hearing. It's called the auditory cortex. Damage to the left temporal lobe can cause loss of language. Injury to the right temporal lobe results in poor performance on spatial tasks, such as drawing.

What Parts of My Brain Control Movement? The cerebellum coordinates balance, movement, and posture. It keeps you upright and keeps your muscles working together. It's the part that learns to play a piano or hit a tennis ball automatically. When you make a conscious decision to move quickly, the cerebellum monitors the speed, direction, force, and steadiness of the motion. The decision itself, however, comes from the brain's frontal lobes.

The cerebrum has a part to play as well. Neurons in the parietal lobe collect data from various parts of the body and integrate movements. Voluntary movements are handled by the motor cortex, a thin strip that lies at the rear of the frontal lobe. Balance is at least partly a cerebral function as well. Neurons deep inside the cerebrum send signals to muscles to help you to right yourself whenever you slip or tumble.

Recent studies suggest that memories of simple learned movements may be stored in the cerebellum. Scientists at the University of Southern California taught rabbits to blink their eyes when they heard a certain sound. They used chemicals to temporarily shut down parts of the cerebellum during training sessions. They found that a rabbit could only learn to blink—or remember to later— when its cerebellum was working normally.

Does My Brain
Pay Equal
Attention to All
Parts of My Body?

No. The more a body part is used or the more sensory neurons it contains, the more space it gets in the brain's cortex. For example, although your back is larger than your tongue, it makes fewer complex movements and is less sensitive, so it gets less space in the parietal lobe and motor cortex. On the other hand, you get a great deal of information from your hands and fingers. Also, they move in complicated ways, so they get a disproportionate share in the motor cortex and the parietal lobe.

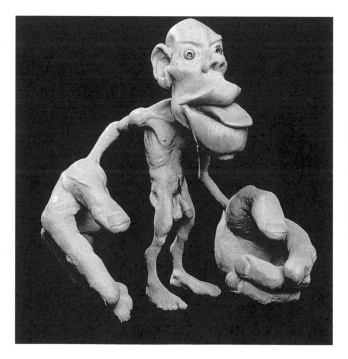

Parts of the body send sensory information to the brain. If they were in proportion to the amount of brain space allotted to them, a human being might look like this.

• 18 •

The easiest way to answer that question is to look at an example. When you're well, your body temperature stays very close to 98.6° Fahrenheit (37° Celsius), whether you're playing basketball in an overheated gym or sleeping in the stands at an ice hockey game in a snowstorm. Your body temperature is controlled by an area of the brain called the hypothalamus. It's about the size of the tip of your thumb and weighs a little more than a penny.

The hypothalamus senses the temperature of blood. If the blood becomes too cool, the hypothalamus causes the pituitary, a gland at the base of the brain, to release a hormone called TSH. (Hormones are chemicals made in one organ that travel through the blood and affect other organs.) TSH travels through the blood and reaches the thyroid gland in the neck. There, it stimulates the thyroid to make another hormone, thyroxine. Thyroxine travels to all the cells of the body through the bloodstream. It makes the cells burn food faster, generating more heat. If the blood is too warm, the reverse occurs: TSH production decreases, thyroxine levels decrease, and the cells release energy more slowly.

The hypothalamus is much like the thermostat attached to a furnace. Just as a thermostat senses temperature and turns the furnace on or off, the hypothalamus regulates the body's energy use and keeps the balance just right. Such a control process is called feedback.

The hypothalamus works in the same way to control hunger and thirst. Tiny receptors detect the amounts of glucose (a simple sugar) and salt in the blood. If glucose dips too low, you feel hungry. If salt gets high, you feel thirsty.

The hypothalamus also directs the "master gland," the pituitary, using both electrical and chemical messages. For example, the pituitary makes a hormone called somatotropin that causes bone and muscle to grow. The pituitary also controls the levels and cycling of sex hormones.

How Did My Brain Grow Before I Was Born?

Brain development starts about three weeks after egg and sperm unite. In the next eight months, nearly all the neurons that person is ever going to have are formed. At some stages, nerve cell division is so rapid that 250,000 new neurons form every minute.[8] As many as half these neurons die before birth, perhaps getting rid of faulty connections.[9] Before birth, the brain grows to two-thirds of its adult size, but only about 10 percent of its eventual weight.[10]

Is My Brain the Same Now as When I Was Born?

Definitely not. Although few new nerve cells form after birth, brain growth is rapid. Much of that growth is in the glial cells that support neurons and in the myelin, a soft, white, fatty material that wraps around neurons. Also, the number of spines on nerve cells increases rapidly. These spines grow on neuronal projections called dendrites, which pick up impulses from other neurons. More spines mean more possible connections in the brain's neural network. The number of new dendrites being formed increases after birth and stays high between the ages of four and ten. Such rapid growth requires food. By the age of two, a child's brain has twice as many connections between neurons and uses twice as much food energy as an adult's.[11]

Experiments suggest that early learning contributes to brain development. In a famous series of experiments, rats were reared in three different environments: some in solitary confinement with a minimum of stimulation; some in a standard laboratory cage with two other rats; others in an enriched environment in a cage fitted with toys and an opportunity to interact with eleven other rats. Later, the rats' brains were examined. Those raised in the enriched environment had more projections growing from the neurons in their brains. Their cortices were thicker and weighed more. Levels of important brain chemicals were higher, and the rats learned better, too. The importance of environment and experience holds for humans as well. Researchers at Baylor University have found that children deprived of touch, play, and interaction with others have brains 20 to 30 percent smaller than normal for their age.[12]

How Did My Brain Change as I Was Growing Up?

At about the age of eleven, the formation of new neural connections slows down and one of two things happens. If the connection is useful, it becomes permanent. If it's not, it's likely to be eliminated. Scientists call the latter process pruning. "The brain is like a gardener who sows more seeds than he needs, then thins out all but the strongest plants. In the brain, it's not green shoots that are weeded out, but the connections between neurons. . . . (This process) is crucial to the proper functioning of the nervous system."[13]

One good example of pruning is language. During its first few weeks of life, a babbling baby utters almost every sound of every known language. Later, as the child masters a single language, the ability to make some sounds vanishes. That's why a Japanese adult has trouble learning the sounds of *l* and *r* in English. One who learns both Japanese and English in childhood has no trouble with those sounds. Pruning may be the reason why children can learn to play an instrument or speak a foreign language more easily than adults.

Human brain development continues throughout life. Learning forges new connections in the neural network no matter what your age. The bad news for couch potatoes and homework dodgers is this: It's not just your muscles that are getting soft and flabby. It's your brain as well.[14] The good news for everyone is that we can improve our brains throughout life: "We can literally change our brain for the better as a result of new interests and the development of new talents. What a marvelous opportunity and awesome responsibility!"[15]

Does My Brain Need Food?

Absolutely. Brains use a lot of energy. Although your brain is only about 2 percent of your body weight, it uses 20 percent of the oxygen you breathe and 20 percent of the energy from the food you eat.[16] With more than 100,000 chemical reactions happening in the brain every second, the brain can burn as many calories during intense concentration as the muscles do during physical exercise.[17]

What Part of My Brain Wakes Me Up and Keeps Me Awake?

The next time a ringing telephone or a crying baby wakes you in the night, say thank-you to several parts of your brain. The hypothalamus, part of the limbic system, gets involved in sleeping and waking. So, too, does the thalamus, located just above the hypothalamus. It's your arousal system—a dispatching center—where inputs from all parts of the body are monitored and relayed to the cortex. Another region of the brain stem, the locus coeruleus, can alert the cortex during sleep, but only when you're not dreaming.

Think about the big job the brain has to do—sleeping or awake—to manage all the information coming in continuously through your senses. If you reacted to everything, you would be totally disorganized. The thalamus filters out messages, deciding which to stop and which to pass along for action. So, too, does the reticular formation, a tangle of densely packed neurons located in the center of the brain stem. Signals traveling from the reticular formation to the cortex keep you awake and alert and allow you to concentrate on a task. The reticular formation sorts the 100 million impulses that reach the brain every second.[18] It lets only "the essential, the unusual and the dangerous" get through.[19]

A question of greater interest to insomniacs is: "What makes the brain sleep?" Scientists at Harvard have identified a sleep command center in rats, and they think people may have one, too. A small cluster of cells in the hypothalamus sends inhibitory messages to the wakefulness centers. "This one little cluster," says researcher Clifford Saper, "has the properties of a master switch that can turn off all the arousal systems in the brain."[20]

Is There a Part of My Brain That Makes Decisions?

Maybe. Certain cells in the cerebral cortex appear to be active only when decisions are made. For example, train a monkey to touch an object and receive a reward of food. Moving the monkey's arm or touching its hand produces no activity in those particular areas, nor does the sight of the lever that provides the animal with its reward. Only when the monkey decides to press the lever do these particular neurons fire. One column of cells goes to work when the arm begins to reach out, another when the hand presses the lever, still another as the animal looks for its reward.[21]

Are Big Brains Better Than Small Brains?

Not really, not even when body size is taken into account. Take humans and elephants, for example. The elephant's brain is larger than the human brain, but not in relation to its body size. An elephant's brain is about 2/1000 (0.2 percent) of its body weight. A human brain is relatively ten times bigger, or about 2/100 (2 percent) of body mass. Since humans can do more than elephants (like speak and make tools), you might guess that humans are smarter, and relative brain size may be the reason.

This theory is spoiled by the shrew, a tiny insect-eater and the smallest of all mammals. The shrew's brain is 3/100 (3 percent) of its body weight, so—if brain size mattered much—shrews would be smarter than people.[22] Have you seen a shrew playing chess lately?

Brain size doesn't seem to make any difference when people are compared either. A mentally handicapped person may have a bigger brain than a genius; and, although Einstein's brain had more glial cells than most other people's, his brain was well within the normal size range. Brain size doesn't seem to affect behavior either. Criminals' brains are no larger or smaller than scientists' or ministers'. On the average, a woman's brain is about 9 cubic inches (150 cubic centimeters) smaller than a man's, but women are generally smaller and weigh less, too.[23]

How Does My Brain Communicate with the Rest of My Body?

A series of nerves converging in the spinal cord links all parts of the body to the brain. Some nerves carry sensory information from the body to the brain. Others carry signals from the brain to the body. You can lift your little finger because your brain tells certain muscles in your hand to contract. Your brain knows when your back itches because electrical impulses travel along nerve cells to the brain. There the brain interprets the input as an itch.

The brain also communicates with the rest of the body by secreting hormones that affect other organs. For example, an antidiuretic hormone made by the hypothalamus prevents the kidneys from excreting too much water in the urine.

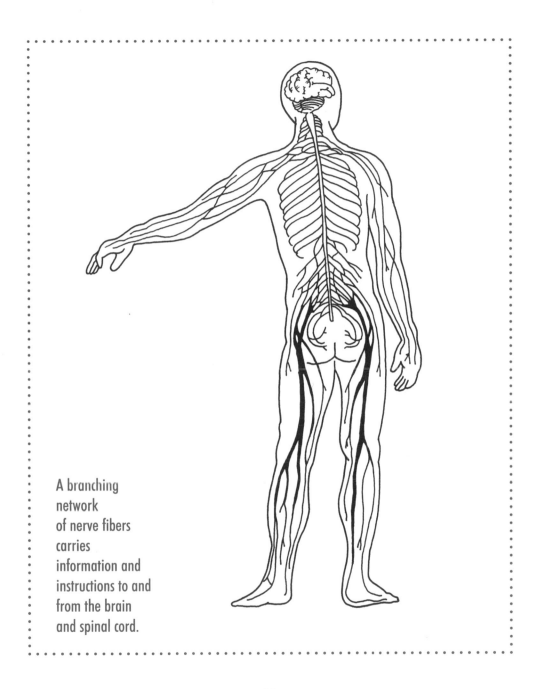

A branching
network
of nerve fibers
carries
information and
instructions to and
from the brain
and spinal cord.

Will Figuring Out How My Brain Works Ever Have Any Practical Value?

Definitely, and some strides have been made already. For example, doctors have developed an implant for the deaf that can bypass damaged parts of the ear and stimulate nerves that lead directly into the auditory cortex. In development are artificial limbs equipped with electronic sensors that can respond to signals from the brain. Soon, scientists hope to find ways to get injured neurons to regenerate themselves, which offers hope to millions with spinal cord injuries and blindness. Furthermore, the medicine chest of the twenty-first century may contain drugs that stop nerve cells from dying, a breakthrough treatment for strokes.

Brain researcher Mortimer Mishkin of the National Institute of Mental Health predicts: "In two decades we may be able to enhance the power of memory through drugs and manipulations such as brain transplants. . . . To begin with, we will be able to treat congenital defects. We will know how to prevent learning disabilities in children, bolster low I. Q.'s, and treat infectious diseases that attack the brain."[24] Mishkin also thinks that research will point the way to curing or preventing Alzheimer's disease, which afflicts some four million Americans.[25] To do these things, we must figure out how the brain functions. Says Mishkin, "You can't repair a car without first knowing how it works."[26]

To Sleep: Perchance to Dream

. . . . .

Sometimes dreams are wiser than waking.

BLACK ELK (OGLALA LAKOTA)

. . . . .

Your eyes are closed. You cannot move. Yet you swim with the sharks, soar with the eagles, ascend into space as the sun melts like butter on a grill. Are you insane? No. You're just asleep!

Sleep is one of the greatest of the brain's mysteries. Although we spend a third of our lives sleeping, no one knows why we sleep or dream. One clue comes from the observation that brain waves are more synchronized and steady during sleep than during waking. Maybe that means that sleep reorganizes circuits of brain cells, perhaps something similar to the way fishermen untangle their nets to make them ready for the next day's catch. Perhaps the analogy can be taken a step further. Since researchers have found that sleep is essential for learning, it may be that the brain is actually "weaving new nets" from the experiences of the day.

From the behavior of people prevented from sleeping, we know sleep is essential for a healthy brain. For the first two or three days, nonsleepers seem normal, albeit increasingly drowsy. About the fourth day, hallucinations begin. People may see mushrooms growing on the walls and hear tigers roaring in their kitchens. Later, memory

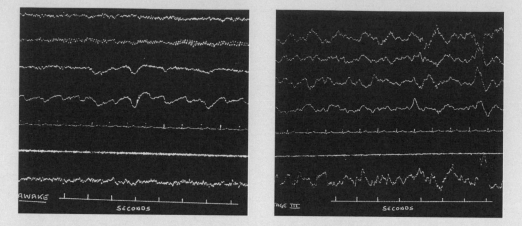

Compare the top two lines in each photo above. On the left is the EEG record of a person who is awake. On the right, the person is in Stage 3 sleep. The other lines compare eye movements and heart and muscle activity.

goes. People prevented from sleeping may forget the alphabet or their telephone number. Longer periods without sleep mimic insanity, but the madness vanishes as soon as sleep resumes.

You sleep in a rhythmic pattern that repeats itself several times every night. In the waking brain, an electroencephalograph or EEG (a recording of the brain's electrical signals) picks up a high proportion of low-voltage alpha waves when you're quiet and relaxed and beta waves when you're alert. But as you sleep the pattern of brain waves changes.

The four stages of sleep repeat each night at about 90-minute intervals, interspersed with another kind of sleep that's perhaps the most fascinating of all: REM sleep—named for the *rapid eye movements* that occur at this time. Although dreams can happen during any stage of sleep, they are more vivid and last longer during REM sleep.

During dreams, the EEG picks up low-voltage waves of mixed frequencies. REM sleep is more nearly like waking than sleeping. The heart speeds up, breathing quickens, and blood pressure rises. Blood flow to the brain increases. The brain

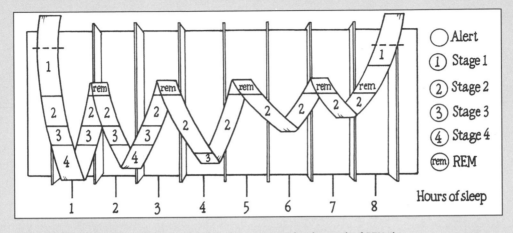

The stages of sleep repeat several times each night, interspersed with periods of REM sleep, which grow longer and more frequent as morning approaches.

sends inhibiting signals to the muscles. Muscle tone decreases, resulting in a sort of "sleep paralysis." This paralysis renders the sleeper incapable of rising to act out a dream.

Do dreams have meaning? The father of psychoanalysis, Sigmund Freud, thought so, and many people still agree today. With practice, you can learn to remember your dreams—even keep a dream diary. Guides to interpreting dreams crowd shelves in bookstores and libraries. However, most brain scientists today see dreaming as a physical process, not a psychological one. Harvard

scientist J. Allan Hobson says that the chemistry of the brain changes during sleep, causing random electrical signals to shoot up from the brain stem to the cortex. By dreaming, the cortex is simply trying to make sense from nonsense. "Under the adverse conditions of REM sleep, the brain is making the best of a bad job," he says.[27]

Still, dreams do seem to have some value in prediction. One study of patients scheduled for heart surgery found that men who dreamed of death and women who dreamed of separation got sicker than those free of such dreams.

Certain EEG patterns that occur during sleep may also predict depression. Furthermore, researchers have observed that people with multiple sclerosis, strokes, or spinal cord injuries may sometimes dream they will get better before they actually do. Common sense comes into play here as well. "Sleep on it. You'll feel better in the morning," is still wise advice to help cope with many of life's problems.

Perhaps the most exciting recent finding about sleep involves learning. No, you can't listen to tapes of Spanish while you sleep and expect to wake up fluent in irregular verbs. But sleep, especially dreaming, aids learning. Scientists in Israel spent the evening hours training people to perform a visual task. Then they divided the people into two groups. The first group were awakened every time they entered REM sleep. The second group had their sleep interrupted an equal number of times, but not during REM sleep. The result? The first group were no better at the task the next morning than they had been the night before, but the second group performed much better.

So much for all-night cramming sessions before an exam. You'll learn better if you follow your evening study session with a good night's rest.

• • • • •

CHAPTER TWO

ABOUT HOW
NEURONS WORK

. . . (might) the brain's attempt to understand itself involve an irreconcilable contradiction? No other living organism has ever demonstrated anything even remotely suggesting an understanding of its own functioning. Why do we think we are capable of such a feat?

• RICHARD RESTAK •

What's a Neuron?

In most ways, neurons are the same as other cells in your body. They have a nucleus, a membrane around the outside, and mitochondria where energy is released to power the cell. (That's where oxygen is used to "burn" food and get the energy out.)

But neurons have some unique structures. One example is a motor neuron—the nerve cell that specializes in sending messages to a muscle and making it contract. A motor neuron has a single long fiber at one end, the axon. The axon carries the signal to the muscle. At the other end of the motor neuron are short fibers called dendrites. They receive

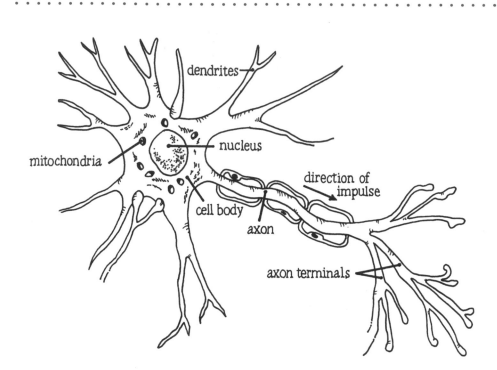

The parts of a motor neuron. The cell receives signals from other neurons through the dendrites. A signal traveling along the axon causes a reaction.

information from the axons of other neurons. Some axons are as long as 3 feet (90 centimeters). But dendrites are always short—less than a millimeter.[1]

One big difference between human neurons and other kinds of human cells is that, after birth, neurons rarely divide and produce new neurons. As a human embryo develops from the fertilized egg, neurons divide rapidly. After birth, division very nearly stops.

Nerve cells of the brain and spinal cord carry messages. Motor neurons transmit signals that cause muscle cells to contract. You pull your finger away from a hot stove because messages traveling through motor neurons reach the muscles of your hand—even before your brain knows what's happened. Automatic responses of this kind are called reflexes.

Sensory neurons do a different job. They collect information from the environment or from other nerve cells. For example, when you burn your finger, the sensations of heat and pain start as impulses in sensory neurons in your injured hand. From there, the messages travel, and can be picked up by other nerve cells, although nerve cells do not touch (see next question). That's how your brain ends up knowing you've burned your finger.

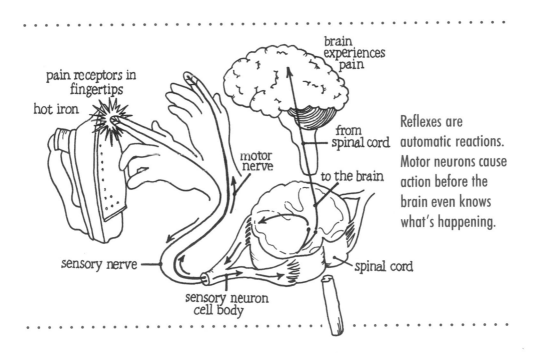

brain experiences pain

pain receptors in fingertips

hot iron

from spinal cord

motor nerve

to the brain

sensory nerve

sensory neuron cell body

spinal cord

Reflexes are automatic reactions. Motor neurons cause action before the brain even knows what's happening.

Interneurons, a third type of nerve cell, are the "go-betweens." In the spinal cord, one of the jobs of interneurons is to pass messages between sensory and motor neurons and among themselves.

Glial cells—which make up an estimated 90 percent of the brain— were once thought to do little more than provide a support structure for neurons.[2] Now, evidence suggest that glial cells produce a substance vital to strong communications between neurons.

If Neurons Don't Touch, How Can Messages Travel from One to Another?

To answer that question, we go back to the 1920s and the laboratory of an Austrian scientist, Otto Loewi. He knew that one particular nerve, the vagus, helps regulate heart rate, but he didn't know how. To find out, he used two frog hearts. He stimulated the vagus nerve of the first electrically. As he expected, the heart slowed. Then he took the fluid from around this heart and applied it to the second. Almost immediately, the second heart slowed, just as it would have if its vagus nerve had been stimulated.

More than a decade earlier, Sir Henry Dale had isolated from a fungus a substance he called acetylcholine. It could make a muscle contract just as an electric shock could, but Dale didn't know why. When Dale heard about Loewi's work, he wondered if acetylcholine might be produced by the vagus nerve. He got spleens from horses and extracted acetylcholine. It had the same effect as Loewi's vagus nerve chemical. For being the first to discover a chemical that carries a message from one neuron to another, Dale and Loewi shared the Nobel Prize in 1936.

Today, such chemicals are called neurotransmitters. Your brain may make as many as 150 different kinds.[3] Only a few are known, and only a little is understood about their functions. Table 2 at the back of this book lists some neurotransmitters and tells a little about what they do.

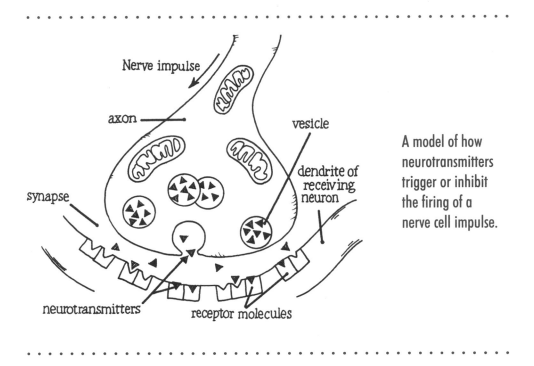

Nerve impulse

axon

vesicle

dendrite of
receiving
neuron

synapse

neurotransmitters

receptor molecules

A model of how
neurotransmitters
trigger or inhibit
the firing of a
nerve cell impulse.

How Do Neurotransmitters Work?

The axon of one neuron, a dendrite of another, and the gap between them is collectively called a synapse. Axons release neurotransmitters at the space between axon and dendrite. Those molecules diffuse across the gap, the same way a drop of food coloring diffuses in water.

When a neurotransmitter molecule reaches the dendrite of another neuron, it attaches to a site called a receptor. Receptors are large protein molecules that stick out from the membrane. They have a particular shape that just fits the neurotransmitter they receive. Think of a lock and key. Only one key fits one particular lock. That's how neurotransmitters and receptors work.

There are two kinds of keys for receptors. One is called excitatory because it excites or starts an impulse in the receiver neuron. The other is inhibitory because it stops an impulse. The neurotransmitter is the messenger, but it is not the message. Its effect depends on the kind of neuron that receives the transmission.

How Do Neurons Carry Messages?

Neurons are sometimes compared to electrical wires, with the messages traveling along them like a current. That comparison isn't exactly right, but it is true that electrical potentials change across the outer membranes of neurons. Thus neurons actually do generate an electrical field large enough to measure. That's why doctors can record brain activity by attaching wires to the scalp.

Here's what happens. A neuron at rest has a slightly negative charge inside it, compared with a positive charge outside. Two factors cause the difference: (1) negatively charged carbon-based molecules inside the cell and (2) a difference in the numbers of sodium and potassium ions. (An ion is a charged atom or molecule.)

This second factor needs more explanation. Although both sodium and potassium ions carry a positive charge, sodium is about ten times more abundant outside the cell. Potassium is about thirty or more times more abundant inside.[4] This difference creates a resting potential—something like the potential for an electrical discharge stored in a battery.

When an excitatory neurotransmitter attaches to a receptor, it causes tiny channels in the membrane of the axon to open. The channels let sodium flood in, thus changing the charge along the membrane. For about 0.0005 of a second, the inside of the cell becomes positive; the outside becomes negative.[5] This reversal in one tiny area creates a current that affects the membrane farther along. Channels there open, and sodium flows into another section of the axon, then another, then another. That's how the impulse travels the length of the axon.

Inhibitory neurotransmitters make the inside of the axon even more negatively charged than usual, so it is harder to excite. They do this by opening chloride channels. Chloride ions are negatively charged. The more of them inside the axon, the more positive ions are needed to open the sodium channels and start an impulse.

To make things even more complicated, neurotransmitters may have many different functions. Sometimes, a neurotransmitter can cause the receptor to activate or turn on a "second messenger" inside the cell, which can, in turn, activate yet a "third messenger." Like lines of tumbling dominoes, chemical reactions in the brain branch, loop, and join in intricate patterns. For this reason, few mental illnesses are likely to be explained by a defect in a single neurotransmitter.

What Makes a Neuron Stop Firing?

A nerve cell continues firing as long as enough excitatory neurotransmitter molecules stay bound to it. (In the same way, neurons won't fire when large numbers of inhibitory neurotransmitter molecules are bound to the receiving neuron.) Also, habituation can occur. The longer the excitatory stimulus continues, the less often neurons react.

In time, neurotransmitters either break down or get reabsorbed. Why don't the channels just stay open and neurons keep firing forever? Because a mechanism in the cell membrane called an ion pump pushes sodium out of the axon, in the same way that a water pump clears a flooded basement.

Can My Neurons Be Excited a Little or a Lot?

The nerve impulse itself is all or nothing. Once it begins, it develops full blown and travels all the way through the axon. It is always the same in all axons except for its speed, which can vary from less than one mile an hour to 270 (1.6 to 432 kilometers per hour).[6]

Transmission across a gap of the synapse is different. It is graded, rather than all or nothing. It depends on many factors, including the number of neurotransmitter molecules bound to the receiver neuron that are active at any moment.

Can What I Eat Change the Neurotransmitters in My Brain?

Maybe, but scientists disagree. Experiments by Richard Wurtman at the Massachusetts Institute of Technology showed changes in brain chemistry associated with food. Eating proteins—such as meat, beans, or nuts—appeared to increase production of the neurotransmitter serotonin, which seems to have something to do with sleeping and waking.

Proteins are made of amino acids. Eating one particular amino acid, tryptophan, may be especially effective in raising serotonin levels. Milk contains a lot of tryptophan, as does turkey. Next time you can't sleep, try a glass of milk and a turkey sandwich.

Eating substances rich in choline may increase the production of acetylcholine throughout the brain, but particularly in the brain stem and cerebral cortex. Choline occurs in egg yolk, fish, cereal, peas, and beans.

Do you have food cravings? Brain chemicals may be at fault. One researcher at Rockefeller University discovered two chemicals in the brains of rats—one that creates an appetite for carbohydrates (sugars and starches), and another that is tied to a yearning for fats.

Other studies offer some support to claims that

- a diet high in fat causes both depression and heightened aggression
- fish oil really is "brain food"—a booster of mental performance
- sugars and proteins can increase alertness when eaten at certain times of the day
- complex carbohydrates such as bread, cereals, and starches soothe away cares

Debra Waterhouse, author of *Why Women Need Chocolate,* also claims that carbohydrate foods produce feelings of contentment and calm, but feels fats lift sagging spirits.[7] Hot chili peppers, others say, trigger the release of the brain's natural painkillers, endorphins. Spinach, seafood, Brazil nuts, and garlic have also been touted as treatments for the blues.

Brain chemistry may also explain why weight-loss diets seldom work. Most people lose weight on a diet but gain it back again later. British scientists looked at serotonin levels in the brain. Dieting starves the brain of serotonin, so the number of serotonin receptor sites increases as if to compensate. But without enough serotonin around to signal satisfaction, dieters tend to overeat. A cycle of dieting and bingeing, starving and stuffing begins. Dr. Elizabeth Clifford of Littlemore Hospital, Oxford, explains, "You stop eating, your biological receptor status changes, you fail to be satisfied with what you eat, you put on weight, so you diet more and everything gets worse."[8]

What Damages or Kills Neurons and Can the Damage Be Repaired?

Drugs, alcohol, aging, disease, or accidents can kill neurons. If lost in adulthood, they are never replaced. However, other neurons can sometimes take over the work of lost neurons.

Is It True that Thousands of Brain Cells Die Every Day?

It has long been claimed that an adult brain loses 50,000 neurons every day and about 10,000 synapses per second, but some recent studies suggest otherwise.[9] Some areas of the brain lose no neurons at all, while others lose perhaps 3 to 5 percent in ten years. That works out to fewer than 100 brain cells a day.[10] Scientists have found that although the brain shrinks with age, cells do not really die. They simply get smaller and work differently—possibly even more efficiently.

No matter how many cells change, a large number are still on the job even in the oldest human brain. If the human brain has 10^{11} (100 billion) neurons, then it has at least 10^{14} (100 trillion) synapses. The number of possible synaptic connections is greater than the number of atoms in the universe.[11] To look at things another way, ". . . if you count them, one connection per second, you would finish counting some 32 million years after you began."[12]

Is My Brain Like a Computer?

In some ways, yes, but with important differences. First, consider these four areas: memory, operation, learning, and doing several things at once.

MEMORY. Today's state-of-the-art computers have, for all practical purposes, unlimited memory. Even older models can be expanded using tapes, cards, or hard drives. The human brain has virtually unlimited memory, too, with no upgrades required, but a computer's memory can fill up, while no human has ever learned so much that further learning is impossible. Like a computer, the brain stores memories in several places, something like making a back-up file. Memory storage is not the same, however. Computers store memory in an orderly way, like neatly labeled file folders alphabetized in tidy cabinets. Human brains are messier. Your brain stores odd bits and scraps, duplicates, dreams and imaginings—all just waiting to be linked in unpredictable ways.

Forgetting is different, too. Brains can do it. Computers can't (at least, they're not supposed to).

OPERATION. Both computers and brains work on impulses. Brains use the firing of neurons. Most computers use electrical signals. Optical computers use light.

The idea that computers might respond to impulses from the human nervous system used to be confined to science-fiction. No longer. Ron Gordon, a video-game writer and former Atari executive, invented an input device called MindDrive. Attached to the user's finger, MindDrive lets the computer read electromagnetic signals generated by human skin. If you think "left," your brain sends out a different pattern of brain waves than if you think "right." These differences are transmitted through the skin to the MindDrive sensor and translated into movements on the monitor.

LEARNING. Both brains and computers can learn from experience. Specialists in artificial intelligence can write programs that grow and adapt, much as children do as they mature. A computer that speaks is a good example. At first, its pronunciation may be poor; but give it feedback, and its speech will improve trial after trial. That happens with children, too, as they master language.

DOING SEVERAL THINGS AT ONCE. At this very moment, you're living proof that brains can do several things at the same time. You're breathing. Your heart is pumping blood. You're staying warm and upright without thinking about either task. Although you're concentrating on reading, you're aware of things going on around you. Is music playing somewhere? Can you smell popcorn? Your brain is handling all these things simultaneously.

So can a computer. While you're writing a letter on your word processor, your computer maintains its network connection, keeps memory tables allocated, and monitors the power supply. You can even play "Doom II" at the same time if you want to.

Such "parallel-processing" computers are almost as good as human brains in finding different ways to hook information together. Asked, for example, to name the baby deer that was the hero in a Disney tale, you might forget the name, Bambi, but be able to describe the animal and tell its story. There was a time when computers couldn't do that. They either "knew" the name or they didn't, depending on how they had been programmed. Today's parallel-processing machines not only can come up with Bambi's name and description, but also can cross-reference every detail of the movie's production—from the year of its release to the animators who drew it. Of course, a human had to write the program that lets the computer do all that.

As appealing as these similarities are, the comparison has limits. Consider three other areas: thought, reorganization, and self-awareness.

THOUGHT. Computers don't link events the way human brains do. The smell of chlorine may remind you of your local swimming pool, sending images of contented afternoons splashing in the summer sun flashing into your mind. Computers also can link chlorine, swimming pools, and summer days if the programmer tells them, but they won't make the connection on their own. And, so far, no computer has reported feeling content in any season, not even summer. British mathematician Sir Roger Penrose predicts that computers will never match the human brain. "Computers compute, but they don't understand," he says.[13]

REORGANIZATION. The brain has an advantage over a computer. It can reorganize itself. People whose brains are damaged by accidents or strokes can sometimes recover their mobility, speech, and memories as other parts of their brains take over for the injured region. "When you damage just one small part of the computer, the whole thing will collapse," says neurologist and computer scientist James Reggia of the University of Maryland at College Park. "The brain is very different. It is able to adjust its own circuitry."[14]

SELF-AWARENESS. The human brain is the only organ on planet Earth that seeks to know itself. Self-awareness, according to the seventeenth-century French philosopher René Descartes, defines human existence: "I think, therefore I am." Will computers someday become aware of themselves? In the science-fiction movie *2001: A Space Odyssey*, the computer HAL does just that—with disastrous consequences. Will computer self-awareness remain a fantasy, or will fiction foreshadow truth? It's too soon to say.

Imaging the Brain

· · · · ·

*The brain is the most difficult part of the body to study.
We carry it around in this box on our shoulders
that's very inconvenient for research.*

E. FULLER TORREY

· · · · ·

Scientists have several ways of looking at the brain. Ordinary X-ray pictures aren't much use. They can't reveal depth, so they don't show much detail in the overlapping, soft structures of the brain. The CT scanner, first introduced in the 1970s, changed all that. (CT stands for *computed tomography*.)

As the CT scanner rotates, measured amounts of X-rays travel along a narrow beam. As the beam passes through, the brain absorbs more or less of the radiation depending on the density of the tissue. Detectors convert the rays that pass through into electronic signals that are transmitted to a computer. The computer calculates the difference between what went in and what came out. From this comparison it draws a picture of a thin "slice" of the brain. It then puts the slices together into a three-dimensional image and projects it on a television screen. The pictures help doctors diagnose hemorrhages, blood clots, tumors, and birth defects. CT images can distinguish different forms of senility, and they can show the difference between old strokes and more recent ones.

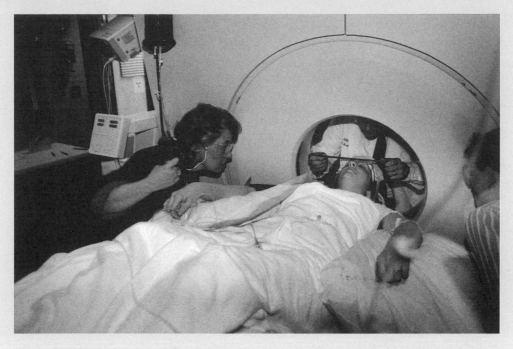

A research volunteer prepares for a PET scan

Another way to look inside the skull is MRI (magnetic resonance imaging). An MRI scanner is a tube that is really nothing more than a powerful magnet. The magnet causes the hydrogen atoms in the person's water molecules to line up in one direction. When the atoms flip back to their original state, they emit a weak radio signal. The speed of the signal depends on how dense the tissue is. From the signals, a com-puter can create an image. So far as we know, MRI is perfectly safe. There seem to be no health hazards associated with the magnetism it uses.

An even more sophisticated procedure is functional MRI. It shows not only structures, but also the organ in action. Suppose a part of the brain is at work on a problem. More blood flows to that area. The increased oxygen changes the radio signal from that area. Thus, functional MRI can show which part of the brain does a certain job.

Positron emission tomography (PET), first introduced in the 1980s, can do that, too. The person is injected with a radioactive isotope. (Isotopes are atoms of an element that differ in their number of neutrons.) As it travels through the body, the isotope emits positively charged electrons, or positrons, which collide with negatively charged electrons in the body. When the particles destroy each other, they release gamma rays. PET equipment detects the gamma rays, and a computer turns the data into a colored map of "where the action is."

Sometimes isotopes of oxygen are used. When active, an area of the brain uses more oxygen than inactive parts, and the difference shows on a PET scan. Isotopes of the sugar glucose—the body's main fuel—can also be used. When a part of the brain is working, it uses more fuel. That shows up on a PET scan as a color difference. PET images can show remarkable detail. For example, different areas of the brain go to work when subjects suggest a use for a noun (hammer-hit) or classify a noun into a category (hammer-tool).

PET has both advantages and disadvantages. It is good for looking at the whole brain at once, although the images of brain anatomy from PET are not as sharp as those obtained from MRI. It is also considered safe, since it uses less radiation than a dental X-ray. Still, scientists are careful about using any radioactive material, so subjects are limited to a few scans a year. Another drawback is cost. PET machines are expensive and not nearly as common in hospitals as CT or MRI equipment.

Brain-imaging techniques help diagnose diseases from brain tumors to epilepsy and from language disorders to mental illness. For example, PET scans of schizophrenic patients show decreased activity in certain brain regions, while those of manic-depressive patients showed increased activity during the manic ("high") phase. Brain images also help surgeons pinpoint the exact spot for removing tumors while sparing healthy brain tissue.

Another major use for imaging is research. Scientists today are using brain-imaging techniques to investigate all types of brain activity, including memory, emotion, atten-

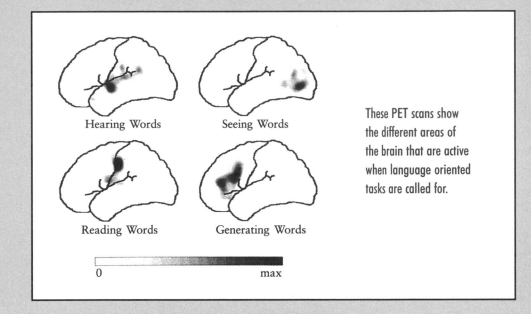

Hearing Words

Seeing Words

Reading Words

Generating Words

These PET scans show the different areas of the brain that are active when language oriented tasks are called for.

0   max

tion, and movement. Using MRI and PET, scientists hope to create complete maps of the brain. Maps show which areas perform which tasks. For example, Stephen Rao at the Medical College of Wisconsin studied how the brain tells the hand to move. Tap a finger, and Rao's pictures show activity mainly in the brain's motor cortex. But use your fingers to tap out a series of numbers, and two areas in front of the motor cortex go to work as well. Just thinking about the same task causes the two areas in front to "light up" while the motor cortex remains silent.

As valuable as PET and MRI have proved themselves to be, they can't keep up with the speed of brain activity. Signals can travel from one part of the brain to another in a tenth of a second or less.[15] Changes in the use of glucose or oxygen are slow by comparison. Researchers are trying to find ways to use measurements of electrical activity or changes in magnetic fields to pursue a speeding brain on the run.

• • • • •

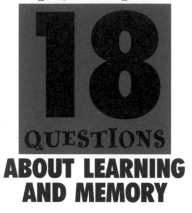

CHAPTER THREE

ABOUT LEARNING AND MEMORY

*Brain: An apparatus with which
we think that we think.*

• AMBROSE BIERCE •

**What Parts
of My Brain
Make
Memories?**

Many (perhaps all) parts of the brain store old memories, but two are especially important for forming new ones. They are the hippocampus and the amygdala, deep in the brain's limbic system. These parts were given Greek names not for what they do but for what they look like. The hippocampus looks like a sea horse; the amygdala, like an almond. We can only guess why these structures are essential to remembering, but one thing we know: you can't make memories without them.

How are memories fixed? Some scientists think that the brain retains memories because neurotransmitters sensitize neurons. A neuron that has received an impulse from a neighboring neuron responds more easily the next time the signal comes along. Some "pathways of response" may be used so frequently that they become overlearned, habitual, unforgettable memories.

For example, what does your best friend look like? Does that question evoke a mental image? Maybe a series of neuronal links has become so firmly fixed in your brain that the image of your friend's face will stay with you for a lifetime.

Do I Remember Best the Things that I Feel Strongly About?

"Memory is fallible in the real world, but stronger emotional experiences make for stronger, more reliable memories," says James L. McGaugh of the University of California, Irvine.[1] Studies have shown that exciting or stressful events cause the release of certain hormones that improve memory of the experience.

Evidence suggests that the amygdala plays a part in linking emotions to inputs from the environment, and such links differ from one person to another. For example, one woman loves the smell of lavender because her dear grandmother always wore it. Another says the smell of lavender makes her angry. It reminds her of a teacher she disliked intensely.

Are All Memories Alike?

No. Some are fleeting and some last a lifetime:

- Iconic, or photographic, memory lasts only about a tenth of a second.[2] For a twinkle in time, your brain retains a nearly perfect image of what you see.

- Primary, or short-term, memory lasts about 15 to 20 seconds.[3] The average person can store about seven bits of information in short-term memory.[4] That lets you remember a phone number long enough to dial it.

• Secondary, or working, memory is the system that lets you keep track of a conversation or work through several steps in a math problem. Working memory involves focusing attention, mentally moving visual images, and calling up your store of language-based information—all at the same time. Secondary memory works for minutes, hours, or days—as long as you need it—then disappears. It succeeds when you remember where you left your keys and fails when you forget why you opened a cupboard door.

• Long-term memory is more or less permanent. Experts estimate that in a lifetime, your brain may retain one quadrillion separate bits of information.[5] That's a one with 24 zeroes after it, or a million multiplied by itself four times.

Long-term memories may be classified by their content. For example:

verbal: language

spatial: the forms, positions, and movement of objects

episodic: times, places, and events of our lives

declarative: facts—for example, that Lincoln wrote the Gettysburg Address

procedural: how to do anything from hammering a nail to composing a sonnet

habit: procedural memory associated with some reward

motor learning: the process that improves movement skills through practice

What Is Amnesia?

There are two kinds of amnesia: (1) difficulty learning new information and (2) trouble remembering information or events from the past. (See the feature "The Man That Memory Forgot," page 66, for a story of the first kind.)

The second is the kind you see in the movies: the loss of episodic memories (the events of a person's life) while other memories remain unaffected. Thus, our hero may remember who is president and how to drive a car, but forget what grade school he attended. In the movies, the loss usually results from some traumatic event, and that can happen in real life, too, although the memory lapse is seldom as total as Hollywood would have us believe.

The most common causes of memory loss are drugs and alcohol. Diazepam (brand name Valium), which millions of people take to calm anxiety, may interfere with producing memories for up to six hours after it's taken. Alcohol seems to interfere with the ability of the brain to use thiamin (Vitamin B-1), which is essential to memory. Korsakov's syndrome, a result of chronic alcoholism, can erase entire decades from memory and prevent the storage of new memories.

Other causes include surgery (as to control epilepsy), infection (for example, encephalitis), stroke, brain tumor, head injury, anoxia (loss of oxygen to the brain caused by the heart stopping or by carbon dioxide poisoning), and neurological diseases such as Alzheimer's.

What does amnesia tell us about the normal brain? If a person can lose one form of memory but not another, different parts of the brain must be storing and recalling different categories of information.

Does a Memory Leave a Wrinkle on My Brain?

For decades, scientists searched for the engram, a physical trace on the brain that might mark a memory. Karl Lashley, a pioneering scientist in this field, trained rats to run mazes. Then he searched for changes in their brains. He never found any. He gave up in 1950 and suggested that memories might be stored throughout the brain.

In 1966, Karl Pribram said that memories might be like holograms. A holographic plate is made of millions of tiny chips. Because each chip holds the entire image, the complete picture remains even if part of the hologram is damaged or destroyed. In the same way, memories might be everywhere and nowhere at the same time.

Another theory suggests that memories are stored chemically. In the 1960s, James McConnell at the University of Michigan experimented with flatworms. He trained them to turn away from light, then chopped them up and fed them to untrained flatworms. These worms learned the response a lot faster than worms that had been fed untrained worms. A decade later, Georges Ungar in Houston taught rats to avoid the dark corner of a Y-shaped box. When he analyzed their brains, he found a protein that, when injected into other rats, made them turn away from dark corners, too.

These findings, tantalizing as they seem, have been difficult to replicate, and scientists debate whether memories can actually be stored in proteins. What they can agree on is that chemicals have something to do with establishing the connections between neurons. The role of neurotransmitters in sensitizing the response of one neuron to another is the subject of much research today.

Also, evidence is accumulating—despite Lashley's failure—suggesting that memories are stored in specific areas. Scientists in the United States and Italy claim to have "photographed memory." Using *positron emission tomography* (PET), they took colored pictures that showed which areas of the brain become most active when memories switch on. They noted lots of activity in the hippocampus and in some areas of the prefrontal cortex. When they stimulated the occipital lobe, test subjects nearly always reported seeing images from the past.

The parietal, upper temporal, and occipital lobes serve as short-term memory banks for what we hear and see. Long-term memory is concentrated in the hippocampus and in the cortex of the frontal lobes. The thalamus and hypothalamus are also important to long-term memory. The cortex of the temporal lobes specializes in the memory of abstract ideas. Certain motor skills, such as riding a bicycle, may be stored in the cerebellum, the part of the brain that helps control coordination.

The prefrontal cortex (behind the forehead) acts as the control center for working memory. It hangs on to relevant information and per-

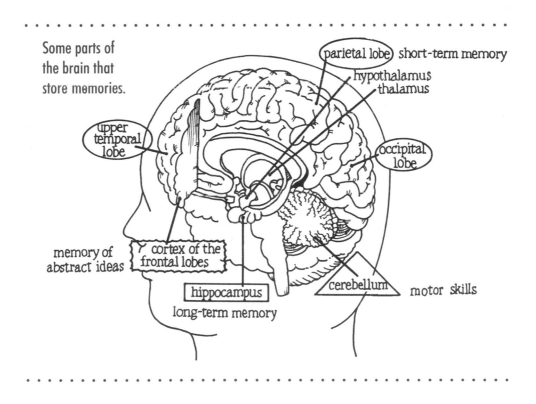

Some parts of the brain that store memories.

forms complex processing functions. The workings of the prefrontal cortex may even explain different scores on tests of intelligence. Those who score highest are those who can juggle several ideas simultaneously in working memory.

Different parts of the brain assume responsibility for memory as a skill improves. Think about learning to drive a car. It's difficult at first, but it gets easier—even automatic—the more you practice. That's because the brain has one set of circuits for handling new information and another set that takes over once a task is learned.

Is It Possible to Remember Something that Never Really Happened? Yes. Highly suggestible people (perhaps 5 or 10 percent of us) can be influenced by someone they trust to remember things that never happened. False Memory Syndrome most often strikes people in therapy who come to believe they were abused in childhood when they actually weren't.[6] The therapist, probably unintentionally, leads the patient to invent false memories of physical or sexual abuse, abduction by aliens, satanic cults, or memories of past lives. The syndrome is suspected when:

- memories are supposedly "repressed" for many years. (Experts disagree, but most people remember if they were abused in childhood. They may even try to forget and find they cannot.)
- memories are clear and detailed. (Real memories are vague and fragmented.)

The whole subject remains highly controversial, especially because it's likely that memories may genuinely be repressed in some cases. Studies at Harvard suggest that as many as two-thirds of incest survivors may experience partial or complete memory lapses at some time after the abuse happens.[7]

Do Neurons Change With Learning?

Ask a scientist what memory is, and you'll probably get long-term potentiation (LTP) as an answer. The idea goes something like this: When a nerve impulse reaches the end of an axon, it triggers the release of a neurotransmitter into the gap of the synapse. When the neurotransmitter attaches to the dendrite of the next neuron, it starts an impulse in the second cell. If this happens many times, the signal is somehow strengthened, maybe permanently. In some way no one understands, neurons become conditioned to respond strongly to signals they have received many times before.

For LTP to work, a signal must travel back from the receiving cell to the transmitting cell, strengthening the bond between them. For years, scientists called this unknown signal the retrograde messenger, but they didn't know what it was or if it even existed. Then they found nitric oxide, a gas that is so unstable, it never lasts for more than a few seconds. Researchers found that preventing the production of nitric oxide also prevented LTP—not just in one pair of neurons but in neighboring cells as well. Another gas, carbon monoxide, has turned up as an equally likely candidate for this job.

So now the LTP theory has expanded to a new idea called volume learning. Neurons line up in precisely organized sheets and columns in certain areas of the brain. The width of the layers is approximately the same as the distance that nitric oxide can diffuse. Is it possible that retrograde messengers, such as nitric oxide or carbon monoxide, not only make memories but actually organize the brain itself? Further research will tell.

Meet **M-R-S. R. R. W-R-A-P**:

M is for mnemonic, a code of letters especially helpful for remembering lists. For example, if you want <u>b</u>read, <u>r</u>aisins, <u>a</u>pples, <u>i</u>ce cream, and <u>n</u>utmeg from the store, just remember *b-r-a-i-n*.

R is for rhyme. Who can forget "*i* before *e* except after *c*" (even though it's often wrong)?

S is for senses. Go beyond what you see and associate something you want to remember with smells, tastes, sounds, textures. For example, you'll do better on a test if the sounds around you are the same as those you heard while you studied. So if your classroom is quiet, better turn off the music in your room when you're reviewing that history lesson.

R is for repeat. Go over something many times and you'll remember it.

R is for rest. Studies show that cramming for a test in one long session doesn't work. You'll learn better if you study over several days or weeks with periods of rest in between.

W is for writing. Make lists. Leave yourself messages.

R is for relax. Tension interferes with recall.

A is for associate. Link something unfamiliar to something familiar. For example, when you meet Mr. Skipstone, remember his name by visualizing a rock skipping across the surface of a pond.

P is for planting clues. Leave letters you want to mail next to your keys so you'll remember to take them next time you go out. Keep a list of things to do on the mirror.

Can I Take a Pill to Improve My Memory?

Do you want to take a pill to enhance your memory, problem-solving ability, or mental sharpness? If you do, there are plenty of people around eager to sell you any one of about 140 chemicals, food additives, or drugs they claim will do the trick. [8] The key word is *claim*. Very little hard evidence supports these sales pitches. "The idea that you can take a pill and fix something as complicated as learning and memory is unlikely," says Charles Stevens, an expert on learning at the Salk Institute in San Diego. [9]

Nevertheless, a great deal of research is under way. If drugs that increase memory or mental performance could be developed, they might not turn us all into geniuses, but they could help people who lose brain power to diseases such as Alzheimer's. Trials to date have yielded mixed results for drugs such as piracetam and estrogen, (both of which may boost acetylcholine levels in the brain) and propanolol (which increases blood flow to the brain). Ampakines amplify chemical signals in the brain by stimulating receptors to respond more readily to neurotransmitters. Several dozen other controversial drugs are available in Europe and other countries, but only a handful have earned approval by the Food and Drug Administration in the United States—and even those few are limited to very specific purposes such as the treatment of Parkinson's disease or epilepsy.

One of the most promising candidates for a memory-enhancing drug is the natural female hormone, estrogen. It appears to boost short-term memory and increase the ability to learn new skills. In rats, it increases the production of acetylcholine, one of the key neurotransmitters involved in memory. Maybe someday women will take estrogen not only to relieve the symptoms of menopause, but also to improve their memories.

For now, however, the only reliable ways to enhance memory are study, training, practice, and effort.

Can Parents Pass Memories on to Their Children?

Not things they've learned, but certain "memories" do seem built into our genes. In animals, we call behaviors that don't have to be learned instincts. Birds don't have to be taught to build nests or feed their young. They know how by instinct. In perhaps the same way, human infants are born knowing how to cry when they're hungry. Such behaviors are inborn.

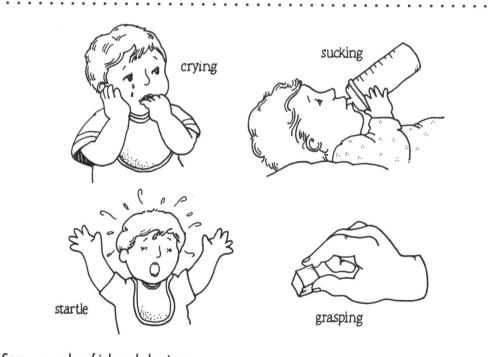

Some examples of inborn behaviors.

What Is Thought?

Many verbs describe the process we call thought: analyze, judge, consider, decide, compare, create, remember, understand, plan, predict, and many more. But we know very little about what our brains are actually doing when we think. Only one fact seems certain: The cerebral cortex controls thought.

Different parts of the cerebral cortex control different aspects of the thought process. For example, people suffering damage to the parietal lobe can visualize a simple problem in construction, but they can't solve it. Those with damage to the frontal lobes can't understand the problem at all.

How Do I Learn?

Probably in several ways.

The simplest is classical conditioning. Russian physiologist Ivan Pavlov noticed a simple reflex act in dogs: They salivate at the sight of food. By ringing a bell before bringing out the food, he trained dogs to salivate at the sound of the bell even when no food was present. The training paired a meaningless or neutral stimulus with an unrelated, involuntary but highly meaningful response.

American psychologist B.F. Skinner took the idea a step further. His method, called operant conditioning, changed voluntary behavior. Rats, given a reward of food for pressing a lever, will learn to press the lever. Reward reinforces a response to a stimulus.

Is all human behavior the product of operant conditioning? Skinner thought so, but his critics argue that many behaviors are too complex to explain as simple results of reward or punishment.

What Is Intelligence?

Intelligence is hard to define. We all experience the feeling of being "smart" in some ways and "stupid" in others. Think about your own gifts. Maybe you're a good reader, but only average at math. Perhaps you know every NFL game and score for the last five years, but can't remember to pick up milk at the supermarket. Maybe you've no love for paperwork, but you're a whiz at fixing cars or broken appliances. Each of us is different, with our own strengths and weaknesses, yet each of us exhibits many different kinds of "intelligences."

Many people define intelligence as the ability to do well in one or more subjects in school. That ability can be predicted from tests of intelligence. Such tests measure several different kinds of talents, including:

· ·

Some puzzlers that might appear on a test of intelligence.

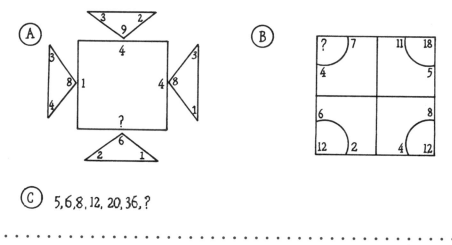

© 5, 6, 8, 12, 20, 36, ?

· ·

Answers: A. ? = 3. The number in the square is the result of subtracting the two smaller numbers from the largest one in each triangle. B. ? = 9. The number in the quarter circle is the difference between the two outer numbers multiplied by 3. C. ? = 68. Multiply the previous number by 2 and subtract 4.

- holding information in memory
- thinking through logical problems
- using words and numbers quickly and easily
- observing and comprehending what is seen, read, or heard
- mentally moving objects in space
- using symbols to make a mental model of "the real world"

Sometimes, items on intelligence tests use words, sometimes numbers or patterns. For fun, see if you can figure out the "intelli-teasers" on the facing page.

No one knows why some people are better at such puzzles than others. We can speculate that the action of nerve cells and the organization of the brain must play a part, but what goes on is anybody's guess.

What Is Creativity?

Like intelligence, creativity is hard to define, but we all know it when we see it. Creative people compose songs, paint pictures, invent gadgets, write fantasies. Each of us is creative in our own way, but there's no denying that some people have "the gift." Why their brains are different from others remains a mystery.

Creative people invent new ideas, or they put old ideas together in new ways. Where many people might see only a single option, a creative person may see many. For example, what can you do with a rolling pin? If you said "roll out dough," you're intelligent, but are you creative? A highly creative person might imagine cutting designs into it to create art, using it to massage tired feet, or to hold the string for a kite.

Inventing stories measures creativity, too. Try your hand by telling a story to go with the art at the top of the next page. If you said the girl is saddling up the horse to go for a ride, you aren't wrong. But is something more exciting going on?

Test your creativity by inventing a story to go with this picture.

Does Getting Older Mean Losing Your Memory—or Your Mind?

Contrary to popular wisdom, most people don't get very forgetful as they get older. Iconic and primary memory stay about the same, although some elderly people have trouble paying attention to two things at once. Working memory declines a little, as does the ability to store new, long-term memories. The death or shrinkage of neurons, a reduction in the number of connections that neurons make, a change in the levels of neurotransmitters, or some other cause may explain the slight changes. Some Canadian scientists think stress, not aging, explains forgetfulness. They found high levels of cortisol, a stress hormone carried in the bloodstream, in people with memory problems.

Some older people do get more forgetful than others. The simplest explanation is that some take on more work and responsibility in later life. Their memories don't fail; they simply ask too much of them. Also, older people tend to worry more about memory loss. An eight-year-old hardly doubts his faculties if he loses his jacket, but an older person may panic about such an oversight.

Studies have supported the "use it or lose it" theory of brain aging. French scientists compared older people in different occupations. They found that those who do intellectually demanding work are far less likely to show mental declines than those in nonintellectual occupations. For example, farmworkers were 6.1 times more likely to be senile or "cognitively impaired" than teachers, managers, lecturers, executives, and professionals.[10] Was this just a result of education? The study says no. The best performances came from those with little education, holding a job that demanded a lot of brain work.

What Is Hypnosis, and How Does It Work?

Hypnosis was originally called mesmerism, after Dr. Franz Mesmer, who first practiced it in the 1770s. In his own time he was both heralded as a genius and ridiculed as a charlatan. In 1841, James Braid, a Scottish surgeon, found that he could talk his patients into a trance. He called the technique hypnotism, from the Greek word for sleep. John Elliotson, an English surgeon, lost his job at London University for using hypnotism during operations. Sigmund Freud, the father of psychiatry, used hypnotism to aid psychoanalysis.

Hypnosis is a mental state in which a person is highly receptive to suggestion. The hypnotist takes the subject through four steps to change a behavior—for example, to stop smoking:

Suggestion: The hypnotist suggests an action, such as chewing gum instead of smoking.

Visualization: The subject forms a mental picture of the act. He sees himself passing up a cigarette and chewing gum instead.

Focus: The subject concentrates on the image and only the image, blocking out all else.

Suspension of judgment: The subject no longer considers the cigarette tempting. He can choose the gum as if the cigarette did not exist.

Hypnotism, continually fighting its carnival sideshow image, has found some legitimate uses in medicine. It can help control the pain of dental work, childbirth, or learning to use an artificial limb. It can also help some people break bad habits, such as overeating.

What Is Brainwashing?

The one thing a brain can't stand is boredom. Deprived of stimulation, it will accept almost anything. During the Korean War in the 1950s, U.S. prisoners of war were brainwashed by the North Koreans. They were isolated from everyone except one guard whom they were encouraged to trust. Their cells were constantly lighted for many days, then plunged into total darkness for many more. The prisoners weren't allowed to sleep. Humiliated one minute, treated kindly the next, they lost faith in their own minds. In the silence and blackness of their cells, they became willing, even enthusiastic, recipients of propaganda they would otherwise have rejected. They confessed to war crimes and helped the enemy in ways that shamed their families and friends, although few brains could have stood up to this kind of torture.

Some cults and political groups use brainwashing to make their members dependent and cooperative. People who lack purpose and direction in their lives are prime candidates for brainwashing.

The Man That Memory Forgot

A man is what he thinks about all day.

RALPH WALDO EMERSON

The man who has taught us the most about remembering . . . *can't*! He is known only by his initials, H.M. His epileptic seizures started in childhood after he fell from a bicycle. By the time he was twenty-seven, electrical storms ravaged his brain up to six times a day so severely that doctors could offer him only one hope: remove the site of the storms—his hippocampus and amygdala.[11] On September 1, 1953, H.M. had an operation that had never been tried before . . . and has never been tried again.

When H.M. recovered, all seemed well. He could carry on a conversation and was nearly free of seizures. But soon it became obvious that something was terribly wrong. H.M. didn't know any of the hospital staff. Although his memories of many years before were intact, his recall of the previous three years was poor. He couldn't remember that his uncle had died the year before. Each time he heard about his uncle's death, his grief was fresh.

H.M. could no longer form new memories or learn the simplest new fact. He read the same magazines again and again. Each time, the stories seemed completely new to him. A doctor asked H.M. to find the correct path through a picture of a maze. Over three days, H.M. tried the test 215 times, but he did no better on the last than on the first; and he never remembered seeing the maze before. He couldn't remember where he lived, who cared for him, or what he ate at his last meal.

"Every day is alone in itself, whatever enjoyment I've had and whatever sorrow. At this moment, everything looks clear to me, but what happened just before? I just don't remember," he said.[12]

H.M. had not lost his ability to concentrate. He could remember a number for ten minutes or more as long as he focused his attention on it continuously. However, if interrupted for even a minute, H.M.'s mind erased not only the number but also the experience of the test itself.

He could learn new motor skills. He learned mirror drawing (drawing while watching one's hand in a mirror) as quickly as anyone else, and he got better with practice. But later he couldn't remember ever having done it.

Further experiments with monkeys gave evidence to explain H.M.'s devastating memory loss. Monkeys missing only their hippocampus or only their amygdala seemed to learn almost as well as monkeys with normal brains. Only the removal of both structures brings about the total loss of memory that afflicts H.M.

Why? Scientists can only speculate. It seems the amygdala connects different senses, such as hearing with sight. The hippocampus links the location of one object with another. Maybe both are crucial to memory formation because they link memories together. Alone, either structure can create a memory, but can't associate one memory with another. Deprived of both, the formation of new memories is impossible.

· · · · ·

CHAPTER FOUR

QUESTIONS

ON THE CHEMICAL
CONNECTION

What the brain does by itself is infinitely more fascinating and complex than any response it can make to chemical stimulation.

• URSULA K. LEGUIN •

How Do Drugs Get Into My Brain?

Swallow an aspirin for your headache. The pill dissolves in your stomach. Then the molecules of aspirin cross the walls of the digestive tract and enter the bloodstream. Once in the blood, they can travel to all parts of your body.

Getting into the brain, however, is more complicated. Coursing through the brain is 400 miles (640 kilometers) of tiny blood vessels called capillaries.[1] The cells that form the walls of these capillaries are so tightly packed together they form the blood-brain barrier. That protective layer keeps many possibly harmful molecules out of the brain.

In order to work in the brain, drugs have to be able to cross that barrier. They can if the molecules are small enough, have the right electrical charge, and dissolve in fat. Aspirin, alcohol, and many addictive drugs can cross the barrier easily. Larger molecules that will not dissolve in fat do not get across. Antibiotics are one example.

Is the Blood-Brain Barrier a Good Thing?

Most of the time, yes, but sometimes it interferes with treatments that might be lifesaving. For example, some drugs that kill cancer cells are useless against brain tumors because they cannot get through the barrier. One new form of cancer treatment solves that problem. Injections of a sugar, mannitol, so upset the blood-brain barrier that cancer-fighting drugs can get through.[2]

Once a Drug Gets Into My Brain, What Does It Do?

Drugs bind to receptor sites on the outer membranes of cells. Like a key that must fit a lock, the drug molecule has to fit a receptor; otherwise it has no effect. If it fits, then the drug can interfere with transmissions between neurons in one of two ways:

- Some drugs cause neurons to fire again and again. For example, repeated firings in certain brain areas account for the "high" associated with crack (cocaine). Crack makes neurons keep firing by preventing the neurotransmitter dopamine from being reabsorbed as it normally would be.

- Other drugs stop neurons from firing. Antihistamines relieve allergy symptoms, but they also cause drowsiness. That's because they block receptors in the brain and prevent neurons

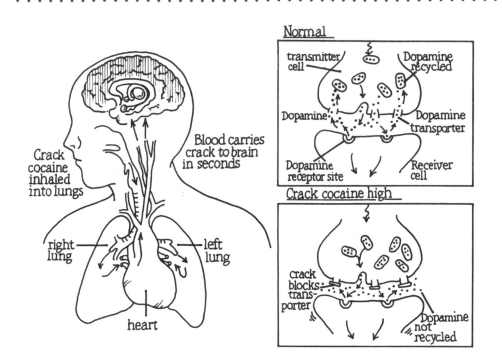

How crack affects the neurotransmitter dopamine and the synapse.

from sending their "wide-awake" message. Morphine, a highly addictive painkiller derived from opium, binds to sites that send projections into the spinal cord. That prevents pain messages from traveling up the cord and into the brain.

The wildly unpredictable behavior caused by many drugs comes from misfirings in the limbic system. For example, drugs such as PCP, or "angel dust," act on the hippocampus.

How Does Alcohol Affect the Brain?

The more a person drinks, the more parts of the brain malfunction. Self-control goes first, as alcohol affects the frontal lobes where plans, judgments, and decisions are made. Next alcohol works its way down into the areas where language and memory reside. With still more drinking, alcohol begins to interfere with the basic processes of life controlled deep inside the brain—emotion, movement, heartbeat, and breathing.

No one knows exactly how alcohol does these things. Some scientists think it makes the membrane of the neuron so "leaky" that sodium and other chemicals can move in and out too easily. Some evidence suggests that alcohol binds to the receptor site for the neurotransmitter GABA, which may explain how alcohol calms anxiety. It may also bind to the receptor for another neurotransmitter, glutamate, causing loss of muscular control, delayed reaction time, and fuzzy thinking. It also appears that some neural pathways just shut down entirely when flooded by alcohol.

How Can Drugs Be Addictive?

More than 15 million Americans abuse or are addicted to alcohol, and about 18 million abuse drugs regularly.[3] What's going on in the brain to cause so many people so much anguish? Addictive drugs act on the brain stem and limbic system as well as the cortex where we perceive the drug's effects. The brain stem controls heart rate, breathing, and sleep. The limbic system is the seat of learning, memory, emotion, and motivation. It also is the source of feelings of reward, well-being, euphoria, or "high." Feeling good is a very strong motivator. Do something pleasurable, and the brain sends a message: "Do it again." Listening to music or playing a sport has that effect. Drugs do, too, to the point where the drug-taker needs the drug to feel good.

Is Smoking a Drug Addiction?

Yes. Everyone has observed (if not experienced) the absurd trap that smokers find themselves in: They desperately want to quit, but cannot. Logic suggests that no sane person would do something that risks heart disease, cancer, and stroke. Yet millions of perfectly sane people light up everyday. What leads people to do something they know can kill them?

The answer lies in how the brain works.

Researchers at Columbia-Presbyterian in New York found that the nicotine in cigarette smoke increases the amount of glutamate in the brain and speeds its production. "The effect of this faster flow," said Dr. Lorna Role, "is like turning up the volume on a radio."[4] The neurotransmitter causes rapid firing of neurons all over the brain.

Every time a smoker inhales nicotine, the brain gets the pleasure message, so the withdrawal of nicotine by the smoker trying to quit leads to lots of unhappy symptoms—food cravings, sleeplessness, agitation, overeating, and mood swings. Deprived of nicotine, one part of the brain demands what another part of the brain despises.

Does My Brain Make Its Own Natural Painkillers?

Yes, the endorphins, so named because they are endogenous (created inside the body) morphines. These molecules act both as neurotransmitters and as hormones. The first two endorphins discovered were molecules called enkephalins. They are rather simple molecules called peptides, short chains of amino acids. Two other peptides called beta-endorphin and gamma-endorphin differ from each other by only one amino acid, but they have very different effects. Beta-endorphin relieves pain. Gamma-endorphin produces violence, irritability, and heightened sensitivity to pain. The addictive drug morphine has one end shaped like an enkephalin.

It doesn't. The brain has receptors for neurotransmitters. Remember that a neurotransmitter molecule fits its receptor just as a key fits a lock. Some part of a drug molecule may be so nearly the same shape as a neurotransmitter that it fits, too.

For example, a molecule of morphine and an enkephalin molecule look nothing alike. Morphine has a very different chemical makeup, and isn't even a peptide. But one end of the morphine molecule has the same shape as one end of the enkephalin molecule. This lets it fit the receptor sites for enkephalin that occur naturally in the body. Scientists have found dense bands of enkephalin receptors in the spinal cord, the first site where pain messages are processed.

· ·

The structure of an enkephalin molecule compared with the painkilling drug morphine.

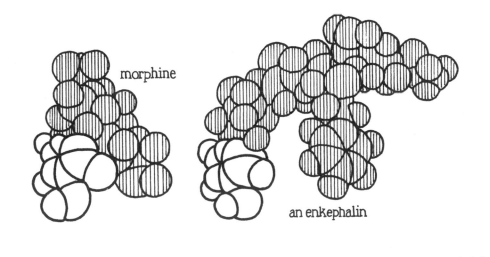

morphine

an enkephalin

· ·

Are Endorphins the Perfect Painkillers?

You might think so because they occur naturally in the body. Unfortunately, they are just as addictive as morphine or heroin. Any substance that binds to endorphin receptors relieves pain and induces pleasure but carries the price tag of addiction.

Why Does My Brain Manufacture Endorphins?

The hypothalamus and the pituitary gland at the base of the brain release endorphins during times of stress. In an emergency situation, temporary relief from the pain of a minor injury can mean the difference between life and death. For example, endorphins may keep a wounded soldier alive long enough to escape the battlefield and find treatment. Endorphins may also promote mothering behavior after childbirth, stimulate the immune system to fight disease, even increase the ability to learn and remember.

Are Sports Addictive?

Have you heard of the "high" experienced by long-distance runners, skydivers, and other sports people? Aerobic exercise can create a feeling of great joy, maybe because the brain releases endorphins. Or maybe the good feeling simply comes from achievement. Dr. Lorin Brown, a surgeon, takes the latter view: "You get so excited by what you are able to do that you feel high."[5]

Can athletes become addicted to their own endorphins? Maybe. Just ask the runner who feels cranky whenever she misses her daily half-marathon. Still, some athletes claim a positive addiction is better than a life-threatening one. Exercise protects against obesity, heart disease, and cancer. Addictions to drugs, tobacco, and alcohol can't make that same claim.

It happens rarely, but there are documented cases of "congenital insensitivity to pain." Such babies are born without the nerve fibers that carry pain signals. Doctors see them most often when they fail to complain about broken bones, open sores, and other injuries and ailments. Two such children, Hannah and Haaris, live in England. Their disorder is so rare, only thirty cases are known in the world. These children can hurt themselves without knowing it. Hannah bit herself so badly that her mother was forced to have all her teeth removed. It cost nearly $10,000 to build a special, padded room safe enough for Hannah to play in. The inability to feel pain is life-threatening. Pain alerts us to injury and danger—signals that Hannah and Haaris cannot experience. "I think the day Haaris falls and cries from pain would be the best day of my life," says his mother. "It would mean I could cuddle him and when he stopped I would know he was OK."[6]

Drugs in History

· · · · ·

An era can be said to end when its basic illusions are exhausted.
ARTHUR MILLER

· · · · ·

The history of drugs goes back to the beginnings of civilization and, undoubtedly, before. We can only guess how prehistoric peoples used the substances that occur naturally in plants or the alcohol that forms in any starchy or sugary food left idle for a time. Records from 5,000 years ago tell us that the oldest culture, Sumeria (today Iran), grew the poppy for opium and called it the joy plant.

Five centuries before Christ, the Scythians of Eastern Europe used marijuana. Ancient Egyptians, Hebrews, and Greeks considered alcohol a gift from the gods, and the Incas of South America chewed coca leaves, the source of today's cocaine.

Throughout history, drugs have been a blessing to some, a bane to others. Certain Indian tribes of Mexico and South America have long used hallucinogenic mushrooms and cacti in their religious ceremonies, but the Spanish conquistadors who invaded their lands considered the drugs tools of the devil.

The history of drug use in the modern world begins with a German youth, Friedrich Sertürner, who worked as a chemist's assistant. He discovered morphine in 1806 when he accidentally altered opium to form a white powder that induced sleep. He named the drug after Morpheus, the Greek god of dreams. Morphine, ten times more potent than opium, was widely used to ease the pain of soldiers wounded in the U.S. Civil War. Doctors unintentionally created thousands of addicts who were free to continue their addiction after the war was over, as tonics containing opium and morphine were widely available over-the-counter until 1914.

Cocaine was isolated about 1860 by chemists who noticed South American Indians chewing coca leaves for pleasure. No one paid much attention to cocaine until the 1880s when the psychiatrist Sigmund Freud began to use it. He took cocaine regularly to combat depression and indigestion. He thought morphine addicts could break their habit by substituting cocaine, and the drug was a sure cure for alcoholism in his view. Freud said that cocaine "strengthens the weak and makes them forget their misfortune." Manufacturers were soon adding it to tonics and wine. It was a key ingredient in the original Coca-Cola.

Freud came to recognize his error, but by then it was too late. Sniffing cocaine was all the rage in the 1880s and again during World War I. By the 1920s, the sad truth about cocaine became clear. Its effects include hallucinations, insanity, and death.

Heroin was a relative latecomer to the drug scene. In 1898, chemists at a dye works in Bavaria turned morphine into a painkilling drug eight times more powerful than morphine. They were so happy with what they called their *hero*ic product that they named it *heroin*. It, too, was available in drugstore medicines until 1914 with disastrous results. It is far more addictive than morphine.

Amphetamines (speed) were the drug of choice in World War II, when soldiers took Benzedrine to stay awake, keep moving, and lift sagging spirits. Such "uppers" later surrendered their popularity to "downers"—the barbiturates and related tranquilizers that promised to soothe the frazzled nerves of workers pursuing the Great American Dream in the 1950s.

Albert Hoffmann, an employee of a drug company in Basel, Switzerland, discovered LSD in 1938. It was not widely used until the 1960s, when it was employed along with psychotherapy in some mental hospitals. When the drug found its way into the popular culture, it became the focal point of the "turn on, tune in, and drop out" generation. The LSD "trip" seemed thrilling at first, but it soon showed its true colors. Especially in unstable or depressed people, LSD can produce horrifying hallucinations.

In 1973, while heroin addiction was plaguing thousands of soldiers fighting an unpopular war in Vietnam, a graduate student at Johns Hopkins in Baltimore made a startling discovery. Candace Pert, working with her professor Solomon Snyder, found the receptors that bind morphine in the brain. She located them in parts of the brain known to send signals of chronic pain and also deep in the limbic system where emotions are controlled.

No one understood why the brain should have morphine receptors until 1975. That year, John Hughes and Hans Kosterlitz at the University of Aberdeen in Scotland isolated a substance from the brains of pigs that acted like morphine. They named it enkephalin, meaning "in the head."

Later, other researchers found out what enkephalins do. Descending projections from the brain end in interneurons in the spinal cord that contain enkephalins. When a pain signal arrives at the spinal cord, the interneurons release enkephalins, which bind both to the neurons that carry the incoming pain signal and to those that would otherwise send it on to the brain. The pain signal is, in effect, stopped before it ever reaches the brain.

Several other morphine-like chemicals made naturally in the brain have now been discovered. Together they are called endorphins. There may be twenty or more of them. All are chains of amino acids (called peptides). Beta-endorphin, which is found in camels and other animals, is forty-eight times more powerful than morphine.[7]

Thus, the brain manufactures its own painkillers. These same chemicals can create feelings of happiness and well-being. The brain makes them under specific circumstances and in measured amounts, and their effects can be important to survival. For example, the brain makes endorphins during childbirth, helping the woman bear the pain and feel good about her new baby after labor is over. That's how the brain itself can chemically alter mood.

But what happens when we take mood-changing into our own hands? Too often, lives are ruined or lost to drugs available today in a dizzying variety. Yes, we can trick our brains into changing their view of reality, but at what cost?

Drugs users who have kicked the habit and returned "from the other side" say the price is too high. One cocaine user confesses: "I'd realized that I hadn't been outside of my house for a couple of days and hadn't called anybody. I wouldn't answer my mail for months at a time." Another person observed: "My perception of everything was such that I no longer had any clear picture of what was going on. The complete inability to really have any awareness of what was actually happening and having to live in a world where I could only feel what seemed to be happening was the most horrifying thing I ever experienced."[8]

Perhaps one speed user said it best. "I think when you're using the drug, it's real easy to deny everything that's going on, and put everything on the shelf, and not cope with it. Your whole world becomes the acquiring of whatever drug you happen to be using. But when you stop, it's all there to meet you. And you have to deal with it, eventually."[9]

. . . . .

CHAPTER FIVE

20
QUESTIONS

ABOUT
WHEN THINGS
GO WRONG

. . . we collude with our illnesses; we invent how we live them.
• STEVE FISHMAN •

**Can Brain
Damage
Change
Personality?**

Travel back in time to find out.

On September 4, 1848, Phineas Gage was working as foreman of a railway crew in Vermont. The team needed to blast a rock. Phineas volunteered to set the charge, but he forgot to pour a protective layer of sand over the gunpowder before he began packing it down into the hole. Gage rammed a steel tamping rod into the hole. Metal scraped against stone. Sparks flew. The gunpowder exploded, driving the 13-pound, 3.5 foot (6-kilogram, 105-centimeter) rod through Gage's brain. The rod landed 50 yards (46 meters) away and threw Phineas in the opposite direction.

The crew rushed to their amiable young foreman. He went into convulsions, but soon recovered and began talking. He rode in an oxcart back to town and was given a room above the local tavern. So sure seemed Gage's death, the townspeople hired a local cabinetmaker to build his coffin. But that evening, Gage told friends he would return to work soon. Despite an infection of the wound and a high fever, Gage was up and dressed within three weeks.

That's where the happy story ends. Gone was the friendly, kind, conscientious Gage his crew had known. In his place walked a man who cursed unceasingly, lied to his friends, reneged on his promises, and burst into rages. He was still intelligent and his memory was fine, but he had lost all respect for other people. He could not be trusted and could not hold a job. He ended up wandering with traveling shows, exhibiting himself as a curiosity at county fairs.

The transformation fascinated Dr. John Harlow, one of Gage's physicians. He wrote two articles about Gage for scientific journals. This was the time when scientists were first beginning to suspect that specific areas of the brain handled language, movement, and vision. Dr. Harlow suggested that Gage's case proved that moral reasoning and social behavior were localized in a single spot in the brain as well. Scientists scoffed at Harlow's idea, but he persisted in his belief.

Five years after Gage died, Harlow asked the family for permission to exhume Gage's body. They granted his request. The skull and tamping rod were sent to Harvard University where they remained on display until 1993.

That's when Dr. Hanna Damasio of the University of Iowa got into the act. Working from photographs of the skull, she and her coworkers used a computer to create a three-dimensional picture of Gage's brain injuries. Performing a sort of "digital autopsy," the scientists looked for the path through the brain that the rod must have taken. Their conclusion? The rod damaged certain parts of Gage's frontal lobes.

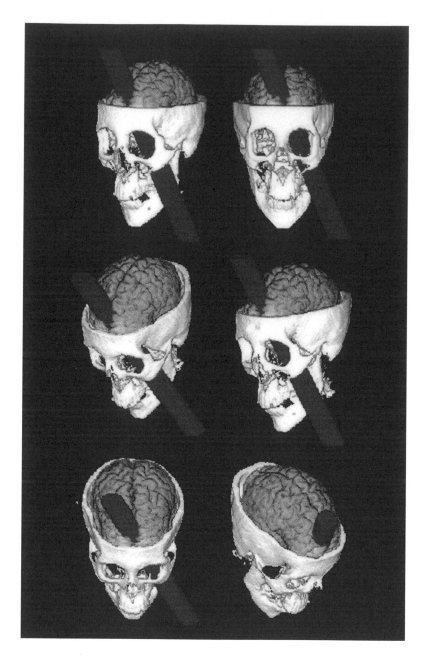

A computer
reconstruction
of the damage
to the brain of
Phineas Gage.

Dr. Damasio and her scientist husband, Antonio, have studied other patients who, like Gage, have suffered damage to the frontal lobes. They behave much the same as Gage did. They have trouble handling their emotions and making personal and social decisions. They talk normally and perform well on tests of intelligence, logic, and memory. "But when it comes to being rational in their personal and social behavior, they just fall apart," Dr. Damasio says.[1]

What Is Epilepsy and How Is It Treated?

Epilepsy is the term applied to several kinds of seizure disorders that affect about one in every 100 people.[2] Seizures happen when the brain's electrical system briefly goes haywire, sending a storm of electrical signals to one area or throughout the entire brain.

Seizures can take different forms. Sometimes, people with epilepsy don't lose consciousness, but they may see, hear, or smell things that aren't real and may lose control of body movements. Another type of seizure makes people unaware of their actions, wandering about aimlessly or making strange noises. The seizure may involve repetitious movements such as blinking or twitching the arms or face. The most dramatic seizures bring on loss of consciousness, a stiffening of the body, abnormal breathing, or loss of bowel and bladder control.

Some people have severe seizures that can result in physical injuries, but in most, seizures are not as frightening as they may appear. The brain actually makes chemicals that stop its own seizures. People with epilepsy aren't in danger of swallowing their tongues, as some believe. The best approach to a seizure is to stay calm, patient, and alert. If breathing is blocked or a seizure lasts more than five minutes, call an ambulance.

In about 70 percent of cases, the cause is unknown.[3] The rest result from brain damage at birth, brain tumors, head injuries, strokes, poisoning, drugs, alcohol, and infections. Some studies suggest that seizures may have something to do with a deficiency of GABA. This neurotransmitter acts like a brake in normal brains, slowing down the firing of neurons.

Nearly 85 percent of all people with epilepsy can remain completely or partly free of seizures with the help of drugs. Some children seem to outgrow it. In severe cases, surgery may be needed.

If Part of the Brain Is Damaged, Can Another Part Take Over?

Sometimes the answer is yes, although recovery is less likely in adults than in children. For example, to treat severe cases of epilepsy, surgeons sometimes remove an entire hemisphere of a child's brain (something they would never do in an adult). Children who recover from such operations often show only slight impairments, such as weakness on one side of the body. Somehow, the brain manages to perform both physical and mental tasks using only half its normal capacity.

Recovery of lost abilities also happens in some adults who suffer strokes, but progress is slow and less dramatic than in children. Although new neurons can't form in adulthood, existing neurons can sprout new dendrites. And healthy parts of the brain can take over functions previously performed by a damaged area. That's why physical and occupational therapy can be of so much help, no matter what the person's injury or age.

Is Stress "All in My Head?"

Yes, in the sense that the brain triggers your body's responses to stressful situations.

What is the stress reaction? You tense, then relax. Your heart pounds. Your mouth goes dry. Butterflies wiggle in your stomach, and your hands get clammy. This is the "emergency reaction"—an inborn response that prepares you for the unexpected. All systems are "go" for dealing with a threat—real or perceived. In an emergency, you are capable of feats of strength and endurance you might never have thought possible.

The limbic system triggers this "fight-or-flight" reaction. Chemical signals from the hypothalamus instruct the pituitary gland to release ACTH (adrenocorticotropic hormone). This substance travels through the bloodstream to the adrenal glands, located on top of the kidneys near the small of the back. The adrenals pump out still more stress hormones with a variety of results:

- Stored fat is rapidly changed to sugar, so the body is fueled for quick action.

- The heart pumps faster, blood pressure rises, and the pupils of the eyes dilate.

- Bronchial tubes in the lungs relax for deeper breathing.

- The digestive process slows down to increase blood supply to the muscles.

- Blood chemistry changes to make clotting easier should the body be wounded.

Fight-or-flight was essential to survival in a time when physical danger might lurk behind every boulder, but what about today? Faced with the prospect of a job interview or a blind date, we react the same way our ancestors did to a charging rhino. In modern society, we detect far more potential "emergency situations" than we ever did when surviving "in the wild." Thus the emergency reaction that was so useful for survival has become a threat to health today.

The emergency reaction of the body to stress causes blood vessels in the arms and legs to clamp down. This increases blood pressure. Two neurotransmitters that cause the emergency response are epinephrine and norepinephrine. They make the heart beat faster or in an irregular rhythm.

Every time an "emergency" comes along, heart rate and blood pressure rise, then fall back to normal levels later. If there are too many such cycles, the continual increase and decrease in blood volume weakens the walls of arteries. (Arteries are the blood vessels that carry oxygen and nourishment to all the body's organs, including the heart.)

Blood clots faster during the emergency reaction. Clots can adhere to fatty deposits on the walls of arteries. The fat and clotted blood can form a blockage big enough to cut off the blood supply to the heart. When that happens, heart cells quit working and die. That's called a heart attack.

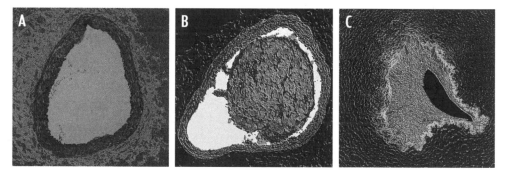

A) A cross section of a normal artery. B) A cross section of a patient's leg vein showing a blood clot, which has almost completely blocked the vein. The clot is made of blood cells trapped inside a network of insoluble fibers. C) Fatty deposits of plaque are seriously limiting the amount of blood which now must flow through that small black opening. This patient is at risk of a heart attack.

Is a Stroke Like a Heart Attack?

Yes, only the damage happens in the brain. Blockages in arteries feeding the brain can stop blood flow. Brain cells that are starved of food and oxygen die. Dying cells release large quantities of the neurotransmitter glutamate. This flood kills still more brain cells. When neurons die, whatever function they performed is lost. That's why victims of stroke show varying symptoms, ranging from mild paralysis on one side to total loss of language, memory, or mobility. Strokes kill 150,000 Americans and disable another 330,000 each year.[5]

Is the Placebo Effect "All in My Head?"

Suppose you take a sugar pill for your headache, but you believe you are taking a powerful painkilling drug. Your headache goes away. A sugar pill can't cure a headache, but maybe belief can. That's called the placebo effect.

How can belief cure illness? Jon Levine at the University of California at San Francisco did experiments with dental patients. He gave painkilling drugs to some, placebos to others. Both groups reported little or no pain during dental treatment. That's the placebo effect.

But Levine did more. After giving the placebo to some patients, he also gave them a drug that blocks endorphin receptors in the brain. The patients who received the blocker found the dentistry painful. The placebo did not work for them. Perhaps belief in a treatment actually stimulates our brains to produce natural painkillers.

Can a Person Live Without a Brain?

No, you can't live without a brain, but you can live without a large part of your brain. The brain stem is the deepest part of the brain. It regulates life-support systems—the circulation of the blood, the beat of the heart, swallowing, and breathing. While other parts of the brain may be damaged or absent and the person can continue to live, death of the brain stem means that all life processes end. A person in a coma has lost (either temporarily or permanently) the use of those portions of the brain needed to respond to the outside world, but that person survives because the brain stem keeps vital body functions going.

What Is Schizophrenia and How Is It Treated?

Schizophrenia is a disorder of thought. Its symptoms fall into three categories: (1) loss of expression, such as monotone voice and blank looks; (2) hearing voices, believing people are plotting against them or that aliens have invaded their bodies; and (3) jumbled thinking, jumbled speech, inappropriate displays of emotion.

Schizophrenia affects about one in every 100 people worldwide.[6] That's more than 4 million Americans.[7] Perhaps one-third of all homeless adults are schizophrenics.[8] Race, culture, or life experience make no difference in the frequency of the disorder, although some forms do run in families. Since the mid-1980s, scientists have located a half-dozen candidates for genes that may make a person more likely to become schizophrenic.[9]

No one knows what causes schizophrenia, but scientists have lots of ideas. Some studies have found that women who have influenza during pregnancy are more likely to have a schizophrenic child. In the Northern Hemisphere, babies born in March are 15 percent more likely to become schizophrenic in later life than people born in other months.[10] Might a winter flu virus somehow affect the brain of the developing fetus? Malnutrition during pregnancy is another possible cause.

A twenty-five-year-old schizophrenic drew this picture to express her feelings.

Scientists have found missing or abnormally small neurons in the brains of schizophrenics, along with a diminished amount of brain matter and reduced blood flow in the prefrontal cortex. They have also discovered abnormalities in myelin, the protein that surrounds neurons and helps them transmit messages. The thalamus is abnormally small in schizophrenic patients, also. The thalamus sorts signals coming into the brain and sends them to the proper part of the cortex. "A person with a defective thalamus is likely to be flooded with information and overwhelmed with stimuli," says Nancy Andreasen of the University of Iowa.[11]

The ventricles, or fluid-filled cavities of the brain, are larger in schizophrenics. That may mean that schizophrenics lose brain tissue or that part of the brain fails to develop properly. Neurons in the frontal cortex age and die during adolescence in some schizophrenics, and some psychologists believe that an unhappy childhood can trigger death of neurons. Other scientists suggest that the pruning of neurons that is normal in the early teens may go too far in schizophrenics.

PET scans show a lower rate of energy use in the frontal lobes.[12] Reduced activity in the prefrontal cortex may explain the rambling, incoherent way that schizophrenics speak. That's where short-term memory resides—the kind of memory that lets you keep track of a conversation. Unable to keep a thought or a sentence in mind long enough to complete it, a schizophrenic may talk nonsense and not know it.

Neurotransmitters have something to do with the disease, as well. While the amount of dopamine in the brains of schizophrenics is normal, the number of dopamine receptors is abnormally high. That makes the brain especially sensitive to dopamine, which may explain the strange thoughts. Also, scientists at the University of California at Irvine found evidence that the brains of schizophrenics may not produce enough GABA. Still others have shown irregularities in the numbers and sites of several different kinds of receptors, leading to the possibility that schizophrenia is not one disease but several—all sharing similar symptoms.

In 1954, chlorpromazine became the first drug approved in the United States to treat schizophrenia. Today, a safer, more effective drug, clozapine, is commonly used. Both bind to dopamine receptor sites and block them. The drug risperidone not only controls hallucinations but also improves memory.

Drugs don't cure schizophrenia, but they do relieve its symptoms. Patients become calmer and more rational and can leave the hospital. Psychotherapy helps, too. Today, many schizophrenics lead nearly normal lives with the help of drugs, counseling, and supervised living situations.

What Is Parkinson's Disease and How Is It Treated?

Parkinson's is a decline in the brain's ability to control movement. The disease causes a slow, shuffling walk, stiff shoulders, and trembling. Depression is also common in people with Parkinson's. More than half a million people in the United States have Parkinson's.[13] Most are in their fifties, sixties, or older. The disease worsens over time and may become disabling after five to fifteen years.[14]

Parkinson's symptoms result from the death of neurons in the brain stem that communicate with a region beneath the cortex. These areas normally control motion by releasing the neurotransmitter dopamine. People who have Parkinson's have too little dopamine in their brains. The drug L-dopa helps many Parkinson's patients. The brain uses the drug to make more dopamine, but the drug loses its effectiveness over the years. Another drug, selegiline, slows the breakdown of dopamine, but doctors are far from finding a cure.

Parkinson's Disease and Schizophrenia Both Involve Dopamine. Does That Mean They're the Same Disease?

No. Parkinson's disease is caused by too little dopamine. Schizophrenia seems to have something to do with increased sensitivity. Other than that, the diseases are probably unrelated. That's because there are two major dopamine circuits in the brain. One is a particular pathway associated with movement. The other is more widespread.

Parkinson's and schizophrenia are not the only disorders that may involve dopamine. Tourette's Syndrome typically manifests itself in a number of unusual movements and behaviors, including tics, poor coordination, impulsiveness, and (sometimes) strange barks and curses. For many years, scientists failed to find any brain abnormality in people with Tourette's, but in 1996, scientists working at the National Institute of Mental Health reported an unusually high level of activity of dopamine in the caudate nucleus of the brains of Tourette's patients. That's an area that governs automatic behavior.

What Is Alzheimer's Disease and How Is It Treated?

This disease destroys brain cells and produces abnormal behavior. It now affects more than 4 million Americans, and that number is growing as people live longer. It strikes one in 12 over the age of 65, one in three over the age of 80.[15] By the year 2050, 14 million Americans may have Alzheimer's.[16]

Although it is a disease of the elderly, Alzheimer's is not part of normal aging. The first symptom is forgetfulness. As the disease worsens, people with Alzheimer's lose their mental capacities inch by inch. They say or do strange things, forget familiar people, neglect their personal hygiene. They gradually lose the ability to speak and move nor-

A normal brain

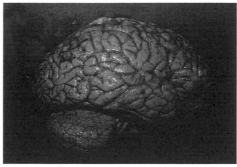

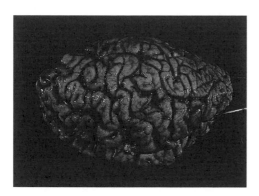

In Alzheimer patients,
brain tissue shrinks in size.

mally. The disease produces depression, delusions, hallucinations, and sometimes seizures. Death occurs in two to fifteen years.[17]

In the brains of those who have died with Alzheimer's, scientists find clusters of abnormal cells surrounding masses of protein. They also find tangles of fibers inside nerve cells. Neurons die and dendrites wither in areas of the brain involved in memory, language, skilled movements, and complex thought. Do these abnormalities cause the disease? Or does the disease cause these abnormalities? No one knows.

Some scientists think that a slow-acting virus may cause Alzheimer's. Others suspect a link between Alzheimer's and the fatty deposits that clog arteries, causing heart attacks and strokes. Still others think that aluminum may be the culprit, since greater than normal concentrations of aluminum occur in the brains of some Alzheimer's patients.

Any one of three faulty genes seems to account for about 8 to 13 percent of Alzheimer's cases, especially those cases that start young—in a person's forties or fifties.[18] A fourth gene is a risk factor for perhaps half the cases that start after the age of sixty.

The body's own protein-making abilities may be at fault. A protein called beta-amyloid shows up bound to dead neurons in the brains of some (but not all) people with Alzheimer's. Beta-amyloid damages only certain neurons, including those that produce and respond to the neurotransmitter acetylcholine. The brains of Alzheimer's patients seem to produce too little acetylcholine. Levels of norepinephrine may be low as well.

We still know very little about how to treat Alzheimer's. Some drugs that slow the breakdown of acetylcholine may help, and a drug that neutralizes aluminum has been tested. (There is controversy about the results.) Postmenopausal women who take estrogen can reduce their risk of Alzheimer's by 30 to 40 percent.[19] Anti-inflammatory drugs and certain vitamins may also delay Alzheimer's or slow its progression. Drugs that treat agitation, sleep problems, and depression can reduce symptoms, but they can't cure Alzheimer's.

Some promising new areas of research include a natural hormone, NGF (nerve growth factor). It stimulates the growth of neurons that make acetylcholine. Drugs that help nerve cells use energy more efficiently or prevent the formation of abnormal proteins may be developed. The female hormone estrogen seems to boost the production of both NGF and acetylcholine.

What Is Depression and How Is It Treated?

Severe depression—what Pulitzer Prize-winning author William Styron called the "darkness visible . . . the shipwreck of the soul"— affects more than 15 million people each year in the United States alone.[20] That's about 6 percent of the population. To make matters worse, depression is nearly always part of the reason behind the 30,000 suicides committed in this country annually.[21]

A related disorder, manic-depressive illness or bipolar disorder, afflicts more than 3 million Americans.[22] It involves cycles of wild, ecstatic "highs" followed by desperate, crashing "lows."

We all have the "blues" once in a while. That's depression in its mildest form, and it's perfectly normal. Depression only becomes a serious illness when a person feels a severe sense of worthlessness and hopelessness that cannot be overcome. Depressed people feel tired all the time. They lack energy and interest in life. They have trouble sleeping and may develop physical illnesses or think about suicide. Some experience anxiety, panic, and despair.

Styron described his own depression as "a sense of encroaching doom" and "a mortal havoc in the brain." He wrote: "To rid one's self of this torment (but how? and when?) becomes the paramount need of all people suffering depression."[23]

Some doctors believe there's a difference between depression brought on by events in life (such as death of a loved one) and depression that seems to happen for no reason. But in either case, depression is a signal that some neurotransmitter system is out of order—probably either serotonin or norepinephrine. Stress hormones, such as cortisol, seem to play a role in depression as well. Because depression runs in families, scientists suspect that one or more genes may trigger the neurotransmitter imbalances associated with depression.

PET and MRI images published in 1997 showed clear differences in the brains of depressed and not-depressed people. A well-defined area of the prefrontal cortex (behind the forehead) is underactive in the depressed. This same area is smaller in the left hemisphere of depressed patients, but not in that of controls.

The first antidepressant drug was iproniazid, widely used in the 1950s. It worked by interfering with an enzyme that breaks down serotonin. Because of its side effects, that drug is rarely prescribed today, but a whole new generation of antidepressant drugs provide relief for sufferers of depression. Some change serotonin levels; others act on both serotonin and norepinephrine. Electric-shock treatment, said to be 90 percent effective in treating depression, is often used when drugs fail. [24]

Are Electric-Shock Treatments Really Still Used to Treat Mental Disorders? Treatment by electric shock or ECT (electro-convulsive therapy) has a worse than bad reputation, perhaps because the idea of being sent into convulsions by an electric current sounds like something out of a horror movie. That bad reputation hasn't been helped much by those few physicians who have used ECT too often or for the wrong reasons.

Today, ECT is used to help severely depressed patients who are suicidal or who fail to respond to antidepressant drugs. Although ECT can cause people to forget things that happened days or weeks before a treatment, a majority of patients in one study believed the treatment helped them and said they would have it again.[25] In another study, eight of nine ECT patients showed reduced depression and no changes in brain structure that MRI pictures could detect.[26]

Is Suicide a Brain Disease, and Is There Any Way to Prevent It? Professionals argue whether depression and suicide result from life stresses or defects in brain chemistry. Some truth probably resides in both camps. A major life change such as loss of a loved one or failure at work may trigger depression in one person, while another accepts, adapts, and moves on. Others experience periods of severe depression unrelated to any unhappy events or circumstances.

We know that depressed people are half again more likely to kill themselves than people who are not depressed, but why one person tries suicide while another does not is still a mystery. [27] Alcohol and drug abuse are often involved, but whether they are a cause or a symptom is debatable.

Differences in brain chemistry point to some possible answers. One researcher found that some suicidal people could be identified by their brain chemistry even before they tried to kill themselves. The chemical 5-HIAA is produced when the neurotransmitter serotonin breaks apart. Its level is lower in the spinal fluid of people who commit suicide than in those who don't. People who attempt suicide but don't succeed also have lower levels of 5-HIAA.

Other researchers have looked at areas of the brain known to bind serotonin. Suicidal people have more serotonin receptors in their brains, and their brains take up greater quantities of drugs that bind to serotonin receptors. Autopsies have found low serotonin levels in suicide victims. Men generally have lower serotonin levels than women, which may explain why they're more than four times more likely to commit suicide.[28]

Since some antidepressant drugs raise serotonin levels, doctors hope that they may also help prevent suicide, but the evidence isn't in yet. In the meantime, the best prevention is still environmental. A study comparing teens who committed suicide with those who did not "found only one difference: a loaded gun in the house. So much for the idea that guns don't kill people."[29]

What Is Autism and How Is It Treated?

Autism is a brain disorder that imprisons its victims in a dream world of their own. Autistic children fail to relate to others. Many never learn to use language. If they do, they may speak in only single words or short phrases or may simply repeat what they hear. They may grunt, moan, drool, stare into space, flap their hands or arms, or rock or whirl ceaselessly. People with autism don't respond to the moods of those around them, although they may themselves appear constantly panicked. About 80 percent hurt themselves, and some become violent and injure others.[30] About five in every 10,000 people are autistic.[31]

No one knows what causes autism, but scientists have found some abnormalities in the brain. Researchers in San Diego compared the brains of normal and autistic children. They found a 25 percent reduction in size in a part of the cerebellum that regulates responses to the environment—possibly affecting reaction to noises and temperatures—and is also involved with movement and memory.[32] Also, neurons in the limbic system of people with autism are smaller and more numerous than in normal brains.

Some researchers believe that neurotransmitters have something to do with autism. In one study, 15 out of 25 autistic children improved when they took a drug that increases the level of serotonin in the brain.[33] Overproduction of endorphins may explain why autistic children hurt themselves; perhaps they are less sensitive to pain than most people.

People with autism perform poorly on tests of working memory. That's the memory you use when you plan what you are going to say or do next. Working memory plays a vital role in social situations. Studies of the brains of people with autism have shown defects in a part of the brain known to be important to working memory. Also, autistic brains are less active than normal brains in areas where incoming information is processed. They are more active in areas that regulate emotion and focus attention.

Drugs used to treat depression can help people with autism, too. These drugs affect serotonin receptors in the brain. The best treatments usually combine drugs with behavioral therapy, in which adults offer children rewards for good behavior. Autistic children can benefit from special education to improve their speech and social skills.

Music, art, recreation, and other forms of therapy can also be helpful. Because even the smallest change is upsetting to some autistic children, they often respond well to planning, routine, and rehearsal of coming events.

Some autistic children need help in adulthood; others grow up to live independent lives. For example, Temple Grandin, who was diagnosed as autistic in childhood, holds a Ph.D. in animal science, teaches at Colorado State University, and runs her own business. "If I could snap my fingers and be non-autistic, I would not," she says. "Autism is part of who I am."[34]

Temple Grandin

Is Mental Illness Inherited?

To answer that question, we need to ask it differently, because a simple "yes" or "no" answer is impossible.

While it's true that schizophrenia, depression, and some other mental illness run in families, it's wrong to conclude that inheritance dooms a person to the same fate suffered by a relative. For example, identical twins share exactly the same genes. Yet, in some pairs, one becomes schizophrenic and the other does not. Genes aren't the only factor. Something in the environment—perhaps even the environment of the womb before birth—can trigger the disease in one twin but not the other.

So the question of genetics becomes a question of probability, the mathematical science of how likely a particular event may be. A family history of depression may, for example, make the disorder more likely but by no means certain. The predisposing genes may simply make a person more sensitive to stressful life events.

Garland E. Allen, a professor at Washington University in St. Louis, says it's wrong to try to separate the part that genes play from the environmental forces that mold both physical and mental health. "The very phrase 'the gene for' conveys an erroneous impression that genes are like little blueprints that just unfold in a very mechanical way into an adult trait. This is not true of virtually any trait, even eye color, because *molecular structure is susceptible to alterations from the chemical environment of the cell,*" he says.[35]

So genes may write the sheet music, but the environment plays the tune.

Can Electrical Stimulation of the Brain Change Behavior?

In the 1960s, Dr. José Delgado and his team at Yale University implanted electrodes in the brains of rats, cats, monkeys, and a chimp. (Remember, the brain doesn't feel pain, so these experiments didn't hurt the animals.) Simply by stimulating certain brain areas electrically, the scientists changed the animals' behavior. A cat would drop a mouse it had just killed and walk away. Docile cats would hiss and attack. Stimulation could make monkeys attack in anger or slink away in submission.

Delgado shocked the world with a dramatic demonstration—not in a laboratory, but in a bullfighting arena. Standing in the center of the ring holding a black box, he gave a signal and a door swung open. A bull entered the ring and charged Delgado. The scientist pressed a button on the black box. The bull skidded to a stop. It fell to the ground, conscious but motionless. Delgado had stopped the charging bull with a radio-transmitted signal to an electrode in the bull's brain.

Can Mental Illness Be Treated Surgically? A number of different types of psychosurgery have been tried with varying degrees of success. Surgery can sometimes be helpful in controlling severe epilepsy. Surgery for the removal of brain tumors also saves many lives each year. The most common form of psychosurgery today is a cingulotomy. An electrode needle is inserted through two small holes in the skull. The needle burns a tiny scar into the bundle of nerve fibers that links the brain's emotional centers to the centers of thought in the cortex. This operation has successfully relieved the constant pain of some terminal cancer patients. It has also reduced the rage and violent behavior that have kept some people confined to locked mental wards for many years.

One rare form of psychosurgery is the removal of an entire hemisphere of the brain, either the left or the right. This operation has been successfully performed on children so wracked by seizures that it is their only hope for a normal life. Because children's brains are still developing, the loss of one hemisphere is not as catastrophic as it would be for an adult. The hemisphere that remains can take over at least some of the functions that would ordinarily be performed by the brain's other half.[36]

Has Anybody Ever Really Transplanted a Brain?

No, not even close. But in October 1980, at the University of Rochester Medical School, doctors took one step in that direction—in a rat! A piece of brain was removed from a rat with diabetes and replaced with a piece of brain from a healthy infant rat. The new section of brain survived, and symptoms of diabetes in the transplant recipient disappeared.

Some success has also been achieved in humans with the transplantation of small numbers of nerve cells. These aren't really transplants but, more accurately, brain grafts. For example, dopamine-producing nerve cells transplanted from fetuses into adult brains have helped some people with Parkinson's disease. The cells produce dopamine, and the patient's movement improves. More than one hundred people have had this experimental treatment, but the procedure is not widely available. Doctors debate which patients can benefit, what brain cells to transplant, what drugs to use to suppress the immune (rejection) response, and how to measure patient outcomes. The technique is also controversial because of arguments over the legality and morality of abortion, although the cells used for the grafts come from naturally aborted fetuses (miscarriages).

Dr. Christiaan Barnard, the surgeon who performed the world's first heart transplant, says that a brain transplant is impossible, given the nature of the nervous system. But even if it were possible, would doctors do it? Probably not. The brain is different from all other body parts. A surgeon can replace a heart, lung, liver, or kidney without changing a person's sense of self. But transplant a brain, and the brain would see itself as receiving a new body, not vice versa.

He Did. Did She?

. . . . .

O, *what may man within him hide,*
Though angel on the outward side!

WILLIAM SHAKESPEARE

. . . . .

In 1935, Dr. Antônio de Egas Moniz, a Portuguese surgeon, heard about experiments with chimps that would scream, rattle their cages, and throw tantrums when frustrated. When their frontal lobes were surgically removed, their behavior changed. They became meek, gentle, and friendly.

Moniz thought similar surgery might help violent patients in mental hospitals. In the operation he devised, a leucotomy, he drilled holes through the skull and cut nerve fibers that lead from the frontal lobes to the limbic system. The surgery often changed people greatly. Some who had once needed straitjackets and padded cells became cooperative and calm—at least that's what Dr. Moniz claimed.

In 1946, an American, Walter Freeman, developed the transorbital lobotomy. It did not require drilling into the skull; it could be done by inserting an instrument around the eye socket. This operation was so simple, it didn't need a surgeon. It could be done by psychiatrists, even general practitioners, in their offices.

In the 1940s thousands of mental patients were lobotomized. In 1949, Moniz received the Nobel Prize for his invention of psychosurgery.

Between 1939 and 1960, approximately 50,000 leucotomies and lobotomies were performed in the United States.[37]

But was this surgical miracle all that Moniz and his disciples claimed it to be? Evidence against it mounted. Lobotomized patients often turned lifeless and dull. They lost their ambition, initiative, and creativity—even their sense of responsibility. Some retreated into a dream world; others became wildly impulsive. Physical deficits included clumsiness, epileptic seizures, and loss of bowel and bladder control.

While all this was going on in medicine, Frances Farmer was busy building a career for herself as a Hollywood actress. By the time she had turned twenty-eight, she had appeared in nineteen movies, most of them hits. Praised as a greater actress than Greta Garbo, she was nevertheless uncomfortable with stardom. She was high-strung, an abuser of alcohol, and the most unpopular star in Hollywood. One columnist called her "direct as a bullet."[38]

In 1942 she was arrested for driving in a dimout zone with her lights on. (It was wartime.) She provoked a scuffle with policemen and a screaming match with the judge. The result was a nationwide scandal and a jail sentence. Her father secured a court order to have her extradited to her home state of Washington. Her mother became her legal guardian.

Her mother soon committed Frances to a mental hospital near Seattle. "And so it was," Frances writes in her autobiography, "on May 22, 1945, at 3:25 in the afternoon, that I was delivered bound and gagged to the state asylum like a dog gone mad."[39] Doctors and staff at the asylum labeled Frances vulgar, uncooperative, insulting, detached, arrogant, foul-mouthed, and sullen.

There, she survived horrors unthinkable in the mental-health institutions of today. Her feet tied together and her hands strapped to her sides, she was left for hours in ice-cold water, a treatment alleged to calm the patient. Her body was sent into shock many times from insulin injections and provoked to seizure from electric shock many times more. Starved, beaten, raped, naked, filthy, and near-frozen, she clung to her pride.

Then, something happened . . . or did it? Biographer William Arnold

The actress Frances Farmer in 1943, being booked into the Santa Monica, California, jail for violating her parole.

claims that Frances Framer had a frontal lobotomy performed by America's most infamous psychosurgeon, Walter Freeman. He states that Farmer was among a large number of patients lobotomized at the Seattle hospital in 1948. He writes of the aftermath of the operation:

Near one end of the row of patients was Frances Farmer. She was, for all purposes, ready to be released. She would walk and talk and breathe exactly as before but there was *a difference. From that moment on, she would not longer exhibit the restless, impatient mind and the erratic, creative impulses of a difficult and complex artist. She would no longer resist authority or provoke controversy. She would no longer be a threat to anyone.*[40]

On March 25, 1950, Frances Farmer was released from the mental hospital. After that, she held menial jobs, played in amateur theater, and hosted afternoon movies on an Indianapolis television channel. She never mentions a lobotomy in her autobiography, but she probably didn't really write the book herself.

Besides, if she had undergone a lobotomy, would she have known it? Would she have revealed it?

Recently some have questioned whether Frances actually had a lobotomy. At least one member of the hospital's staff denies Arnold's allegation.[41]

Records are missing. . . .

Witnesses aren't talking. . . .

Frances Farmer is dead, and the history of her illness has died with her.

Frontal lobotomies are no longer performed in the U.S. or anywhere else in the world.

· · · · ·

CHAPTER SIX

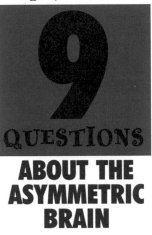

QUESTIONS

ABOUT THE ASYMMETRIC BRAIN

Let not the right side of your brain know what the left side doeth.

• GEORGE BERNARD SHAW •

Do the Bumps on My Head Reveal Anything About My Brain Underneath?

Phrenology was a nineteenth-century belief that bumps on the skull revealed a person's character. Some took it seriously, while others laughed—much as people do about astrology today. Astrology has no scientific basis and, as it turned out, neither did phrenology. The bumps on the skull tell nothing about the brain that lies beneath.

Today, phrenology may seem silly, but harmless. Unfortunately, it hurt serious science for many decades. No self-respecting scientist wanted to suggest that areas of the brain might specialize for fear of sounding ridiculous.

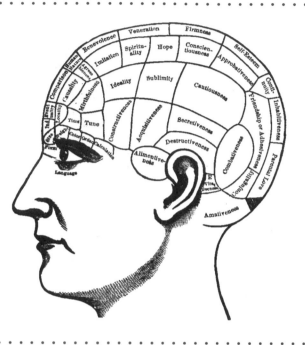

A phrenologist's map of character traits associated with bumps on the skull.

Does the Left Side of My Brain Control the Right Side of My Body, and Vice Versa?

Yes. The first clues came from studying soldiers whose skulls were broken open in battle. In 1870 the Prussian army was fighting Napoleon III in France. Gustav Fritsch and Eduard Hitzig, two Prussian doctors, studied the exposed brains of wounded soldiers. They stimulated various areas with tiny electric currents. (This wasn't as ghoulish as it sounds. The brain feels no pain, and the brains were already exposed by battlefield injuries. The lives of the soldiers were not threatened. Still, such experiments certainly wouldn't be permitted today.)

When Fritsch and Hitzig stimulated the right side of the brain, the left side of the body moved. When they stimulated the left side, the right side moved. They concluded that each side of the brain controls the opposite side of the body.

Therefore, an injury of the left parietal lobe can cause a person to act as if the right side of the body simply does not exist. Also, because information coming into the visual field from one side is handled by the opposite side of the brain, vision can be affected. For example, when asked to draw a picture of a clock, a patient with left hemisphere brain damage may crowd all 12 numbers into the left half of the circle.

Are Right-Handed People also Right-Footed and Right-Eyed?

When you rise from your chair and start to walk across the room, which foot takes the lead? What about climbing stairs? Do you begin with one foot or the other most of the time? Many people do. You may have a preferred foot, ear, and eye just as you have a preferred hand, but the side may not always be the same. Being right-handed makes right-footedness more likely, but not a certainty. Some people have opposite preferred hands and feet, and nearly half of us show no strong foot preference at all.

Eye and ear preferences seem to have nothing to do with handedness. Maybe that's because the brain's centers for processing sight and sound occur in both hemispheres.

Do the Right and Left Sides of My Brain Specialize?

Yes. In most people, the left hemisphere specializes in language and logic. The right is best at identifying patterns and dealing with three-dimensional space. The left handles one fact at a time, one step at a time. The right grasps concepts in their entirety, complete and in an instant.

The right and left hemispheres specialize, but their activities are coordinated by communications across the corpus callosum.

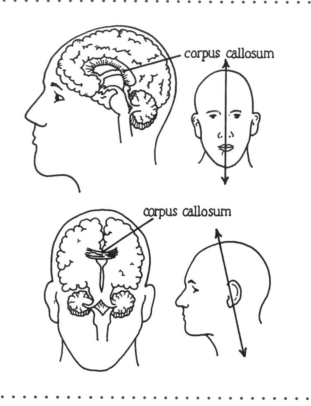

corpus callosum

corpus callosum

In the majority of humans, the left hemisphere is dominant. It serves as headquarters for speech, calculating, and rational thought. This is where most of the work gets done when you write a letter, solve a math problem, or work a crossword puzzle.

The right hemisphere has equally important jobs to do. It recognizes faces and shapes, keeps us from getting lost, and handles daily routines such as washing, dressing, and brushing teeth. It can solve problems through association, but it can't speak.

The two hemispheres specialize, but in healthy brains they work in harmony. Each side knows what the other is doing, in part because messages travel back and forth through the corpus callosum, the bundle of 200–300 million neurons that connects the two hemispheres. [1] Communication across the corpus callosum is so good that it's impossible to carry out two mental tasks simultaneously. To prove it, try drawing a picture with one hand and solving a math problem with the other.

Are Artistic or Musical People Right-Brained?

The right hemisphere definitely has a talent for music. One researcher asked volunteers to listen to two melodies played at the same time—one in each ear. The result? Right-handed subjects better remembered the tune they had heard in their left ears. The left ear sends signals principally to the right side of the brain.

A stroke that damages the right hemisphere may rob its victim of the ability to sing, while speech stays normal. The opposite can happen, too. Damage to the left hemisphere can result in loss of speech, but the person may still be able to sing. People who have their right temporal lobes removed to control seizures lose some of their ability to understand and perform music.

Still, it's wrong to say that music is entirely a right-hemisphere activity, especially in trained musicians. (See the feature "Music and the Brain," page 119.) In the same way, evidence is thin that art is a right-brained activity. The popular notion that the left brain is logical (if a bit dull) while the right brain is creative (if a bit unpredictable) simply doesn't hold up under careful (left-brained?) scrutiny. Nor is there any truth to the idea that logical people are left-brained and artistic people are right-brained.

What Would Happen If the Two Sides of My Brain Couldn't Communicate?

When the corpus callosum is cut, either accidentally or intentionally, some strange things happen. In 1961 doctors in California began severing that bundle of fibers in patients suffering from the most severe forms of epilepsy. In most cases, the patients had fewer or less severe seizures. It seemed that the treatment was successful.

Roger Sperry won a Nobel Prize twenty years later for his studies of these "split-brain" patients after their recovery. In everyday living, they appeared no different from anyone else. They could walk, talk, eat, swim, dance, sing, solve problems, and do all the other things that normal people do. But Sperry noticed that when asked to raise a hand or knee, a split-brain patient would always raise the right, never the left. The left brain might be understanding words, but the right brain wasn't answering.

Sperry did some experiments to learn more. In one of them, he gave split-brain patients a set of blocks painted with different arrangements of red and white on each face. He asked them to put the blocks together to match a pattern he supplied. With their left hands, the patients could complete the pattern easily, but with their right hands, they got it wrong.

Sperry thought he was seeing the effects of "two minds," or "two spheres of consciousness." The trouble was, he had no way of knowing whether normal people are also of two minds, or if the results he observed were side effects of the surgery. Sperry enlisted a graduate student, Michael Gazzaniga, to help him find out.

"My first quick take . . . in 1961 was that one side of the brain did something the other didn't know about," Gazzaniga explained more than thirty years later.[2] He found that a split-brain patient might button his shirt with his left hand while his right hand was unbuttoning it at the same time. Gazzaniga hid objects behind barriers and asked split-

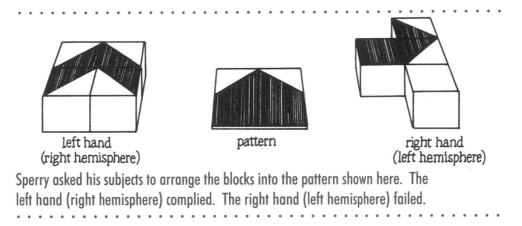

left hand
(right hemisphere)

pattern

right hand
(left hemisphere)

Sperry asked his subjects to arrange the blocks into the pattern shown here. The left hand (right hemisphere) complied. The right hand (left hemisphere) failed.

brain patients to describe them only by touch. He found they could describe a hidden spoon held in the right hand, but not in the left. Yet they could copy a drawing of a solid object better with the left hand than with the right, even if right-handed.

Gazzaniga and Sperry showed split-brain patients two objects on a screen: a sphere on the left side and a cube on the right. When asked what they saw, they answered "a cube." Next, subjects used their left hands to feel objects they couldn't see, including both a cube and a sphere. When asked to match one of the felt objects to what they saw, they chose the sphere.

What might explain such strange behavior? The two sides of the brain handle information from the opposite visual field. That is, what the right eye sees goes to the left brain for interpretation. The left brain is the center of language, too. Thus, the left brain can give a name to what's in the right visual field without communicating with the right hemisphere. But the right hemisphere lacks language; it cannot report information from the left visual field. The right brain can, however, tell one shape from another. Furthermore, it can communicate that information to the left hand with no need for words.

The left brain names the cube seen in the right visual field. The right brain has no language, but it can match the feel of the sphere to the object seen in the left visual field.

How information from the right visual field, perceived by the left brain, tells the right hand what to do . . . and vice versa.

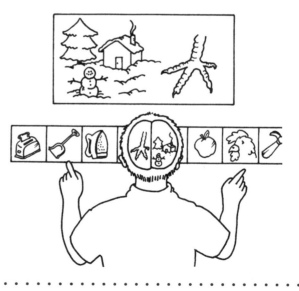

In another experiment, a split-brain patient saw a picture of a bird's claw on the right and a snow scene on the left. Given a number of pictures and asked to choose a related one, he pointed to a chicken with his right hand and a shovel with his left.

Chicken and claw made sense to the left hemisphere, which processes information from the right visual field and controls the right hand. The winter scene made sense to the right hemisphere, which then directed the left hand to choose the shovel. But that's not the end of the story. The verbal left brain invents plausible reasons for what the right brain does. When asked to explain why his right hand had chosen a shovel, the patient answered, "You need a shovel to clean a chicken shed."

Are Left-Handed People Right-Brain Dominant?

Not necessarily. Three patterns of brain organization occur. Two-thirds of left-handers are the same as 99 percent of right-handers, with language on the left and spatial skills centered in the right.[3] Some of the remaining left-handers have language on the right instead of the left, and some have language and spatial abilities in both hemispheres. Whether these differences cause any problems is debatable. Some studies show that lefties have trouble with language and spatial tasks, while others do not. Left-handers do seem to have an advantage in recovering from brain damage. Their brains seem better able to transfer language functions to undamaged areas.

Are Men's and Women's Brains Different?

On the average, girls are better with words than boys. They work better with their hands (fine muscle control) and are less aggressive. Boys generally have better large muscle control and show earlier right hemisphere development than girls. Boys have more confidence in their math abilities than girls, but girls do better on standardized math tests through their elementary and middle school years. By high school, boys get ahead.

Men and woman have different means of finding their way around. Women rely on landmarks and signs, while men are more likely to use distances and directions. Women have keener senses of hearing, smell, and taste, but men have sharper eyes. Women are better at interpreting body language—those subtle messages hidden in the lift of an eyebrow or the tone of a question.

For many years, experts have argued about whether such differences in math and language skills arise from the brain itself or from the social environment. Parents and teachers treat boys and girls differently, some have argued, which might mean that one sex develops a certain intellectual skill more fully than the other.

Others believe brain structure and function may be fundamentally different. Although there is no difference in the size and shape of the hemispheres, the two sides are more specialized in males than in females. In males, the left brain is more clearly the language side and the right more specialized for spatial tasks.

Some differences in structure have been found. The corpus callosum carries messages between the two hemispheres. It is generally larger in women than in men. So is the anterior commissure, a smaller bundle of fibers lower down in the brain. In one part of the temporal lobe, women have about 10 percent more neurons than men.

Canadian scientist Sandra Wittelson examined the way that neurons are packed in the brain. Six layers of nerve cells make up the temporal lobes of the cerebral cortex. The cells are stacked closer together in the second and sixth layers of women as compared with men. These layers process language, melodies, and tone of voice.

PET and functional MRI have let scientists take pictures of male and female brains at work. In one experiment, 37 men and 24 women lay relaxed in a dark room and thought about nothing. (That's very hard to do. Try it!) Both men and women showed greatest mental activity in the limbic system, but in different regions. In men, the pictures glowed in areas associated with aggression. Women's brain work was higher up where emotions are revealed through facial expressions and words. But individuals varied a lot. Four women and 13 men had PET scans that looked like those of the other sex.

Some other differences have shown up in pictures of the brain, for example:

- When men and women of high math ability are compared, the men's brains "work harder" (that is, use more glucose and oxygen) than the women's.

- Men use a language center on the left side of the brain to figure out rhymes. Women use the same center plus an additional region on the right.

- When asked to judge happy and sad faces from photographs, women scored better, but men's brains used more energy.

- When recalling sad memories, the limbic system becomes active in both sexes. But women's brains show active areas eight times larger than men's.

As intriguing as these differences are, no one knows what they mean, or if they mean anything at all in practical terms. So be careful about jumping to conclusions:

- Notice words such as "typically," "generally," or "often." Whenever studies compare groups of people, they look at averages. Averages say nothing about individuals. They cannot predict what any one person can do or how any two people will compare. Draw numbers to choose a boy and a girl, and he might beat her at reading and she might beat him at the high jump.

- Don't confuse "different" with "better" or "worse." The average girl may be better than the average boy with words, but that doesn't make her a more worthwhile person, any more than the average boy's ability to kick a football makes him superior to the average girl.

- Don't get caught in the "nature-nurture" argument. Are boys and girls born different, or does their upbringing make them different? Probably both. "You can't pull apart nature and nurture,"[4] says psychologist Diane Halpern. To attempt to do so is, in the view of geneticist Steve Jones, "like trying to unbake the cake."[5]

Do the Hemispheres Specialize in Different Emotions?

Maybe. Scientists in New York asked people to relive intensely emotional experiences. They found that the left hemisphere worked overtime on happy and pleasant memories, but the right called up anger and sorrow. Researchers at Johns Hopkins University say "worrying" is a right-brain activity. Their PET scans showed increased blood flow in the right frontal lobe when research volunteers listened to taped stories about family crises, financial problems, or stress in the workplace (as compared to "neutral" tapes about flower arranging). "Worrying occurs when no easy solution is available," says Rudolf Hoehn-Saric, director of the university's anxiety disorders unit. "The solution is often derived emotionally rather than rationally," he says.[6]

Music and the Brain

*The mind ought sometimes to be amused, that it
may better return to thought, and to itself.*

PHAEDRUS (FIFTH CENTURY B.C.)

Music can motivate soldiers to fight, rally crowds to a cause, even soothe the troubled mind into sleep. Market researchers know that music in stores increases the amount of time shoppers spend there and the amount of money they spend. New research shows that music may enhance learning, memory, even intelligence.

In separate rooms, three groups of college students prepare for a test. One group sits in silence. Another listens to instructions to relax. A third hears ten minutes of Mozart's Piano Sonata K448. Later, the students who listened to music do better on the test.

Could stress relief account for the improvement? Not likely, for the test was no ordinary exam. It mea-sured spatial reasoning. That's the brain's ability to form mental pictures of objects and move them around in imaginary space. How important is spatial reasoning? Just ask a mathematician, architect, or engineer.

This "Mozart Effect"—the capacity of music to improve spatial reasoning—can benefit even very young children. Frances Rauscher and her colleagues at the University of California, Irvine who first found the effect also studied three-year-olds who had thirty minutes of daily singing lessons. The children were better at putting puzzles together than children who had no musical training.

The "Mozart Effect" shows up in scans of brain activity. Music stimulates areas associated with hearing, recall, and—most surprising—vision. Music elicits some kind of mental picture, whether the listener is aware of it or not.

Training in music seems to change both how the brain works and how it is built. For example, in most adult nonmusicians, appreciation of music tends to be divided between the two hemispheres. The right side handles melody and intonation; the left, rhythm and notation. But among the most highly trained and skilled musicians, music appears to be a largely left-brain activity. The planum temporale, a part of the left hemisphere that processes sound, is larger in musicians than in nonmusical people. It's larger still in musicians who have perfect pitch. Whether they were born this way or early musical training affected brain development is open to debate.

German scientists have found that the corpus callosum (the bundle of fibers that passes messages between the two sides of the brain) is 10 to 15 percent thicker in musicians who started training before the age of seven than in nonmusicians. They think that rapid communication between the hemispheres—needed, for example,

when playing a difficult piano piece—may explain the increase.

Researchers at Stanford University in California think that an understanding of the structure of music is present in our brains from birth. They taught babies to control music being played. If the infants looked at a checkerboard, the music stayed on. If they looked away, it stopped. Then the scientists played excerpts from Bach, Beethoven, and Bartók in two forms: either correct ones (as the composers wrote them) or with pauses inserted in inappropriate places. When the infants heard the correct excerpts first, they listened longer than they did to the disrupted excerpts. If the disrupted melodies were played first, the babies showed no preference.

Plato thought that children should study music to foster order and harmony in the mind. Maybe he was on the right track. Some scientists believe that music builds strong minds just as exercise builds strong muscles. Says Frances Rauscher: "Might music be a kind of essential nutrient that the human brain requires? Can music make us more intelligent? . . . The answer, at least so far, is yes. . . . Music should be prized as a way to boost human brainpower."[7]

CHAPTER SEVEN

13 QUESTIONS

ABOUT SENSING AND SPEAKING

Each of us sees things differently;
each of us constructs a world of our own.

• VERNON MOUNTCASTLE •

How Does My Brain Handle Signals From My Eyes, Ears, and Other Sense Organs?

Vision is the best understood of the senses. We know a lot about how it works. Hearing, taste, smell, and touch (including temperature and pain) may work in similar ways, but we know too little about them to be sure.

The visual areas of the cortex contain more neurons than all the rest of the brain put together. The six layers of visual neurons are stacked one on top of another in columns, like coins. The columns respond to different kinds of input. An experiment with monkeys shows how. Scientists recorded activity in two areas of the brain: call one IC; call the other PS. The researchers found if they kept the object the monkey saw the same, but changed its location, neurons around the monkey's PS fired. The IC remained quiet. But when they changed the object, but kept the place the same, the neurons of the IC came to life while the PS remained inactive.

Visual neurons are very particular about the kind of information they handle. Some respond only to a certain color or to a movement in a one direction. Some detect only pinpoints of light; others, only edges and lines. So precise is their action that one line-detecting neuron "sees" only horizontal lines, while another picks up only edges a few degrees off the horizontal. Still another detects only right angles.

From the brain's vision centers, signals travel to many networks of neurons. This neural networking lets you link information and ideas. That's how, for example, you recognize a friend's face and respond appropriately with a warm greeting. It seems simple enough, but we know very little about how your brain achieves such a complicated marvel.

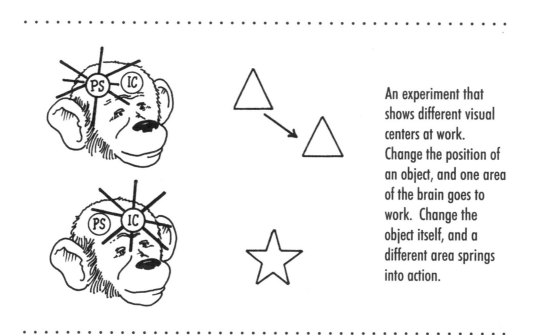

An experiment that shows different visual centers at work. Change the position of an object, and one area of the brain goes to work. Change the object itself, and a different area springs into action.

How Does My Brain "See" Color?

A physicist will tell you that there is no such thing as color in the real world. Like beauty, color is in the eye of the beholder—or, more accurately, in the brain of the one who sees.

Light acts like particles, but it also behaves like a wave. The distance between the peaks of the waves can vary. That's wavelength. White light contains many wavelengths. Objects reflect different wavelengths, but these wavelengths themselves have no color. Color vision is just the brain's way of telling one wavelength from another.

Rods are cells in the retina of the eye that work best in dim light. They fire in response to the wavelengths the brain interprets as shades of gray. Color-receiving cells, called cones, contain three light-sensitive pigments—red, yellow-green, and blue. These pigments change for an instant in response to the wavelength of light that hits them. That stimulates certain neurons in the eye to send signals to the visual cortex of the brain. The brain interprets these signals as red, green, or any other of the hundreds of different shades and hues that the human brain can tell apart.

Does the Brain Organize the Environment, or Does the Environment Organize the Brain?

Both. The brain is expert at seeing what it thinks it should, in finding pattern where there is none.

For example, what do you see in this picture?

BRAIN

If you see the word "brain," yours is playing tricks on you. There are no letters, just some straight and curved lines. Notice how the "bars" of the A, I, and N appear to be whiter than the rest of the page. Look again. The "bars" are not really there. You've had experience with block letters, so your brain insists on finding a meaningful pattern. In other words, your brain is organizing your environment.

Try another one. What do you see in the picture below—a young girl or an old lady? Keep looking. Both are there. Once you see both, you'll flip back and forth between them. That's a brain at work, trying to organize its environment and having trouble doing it.

The opposite is also true: The environment organizes the brain. That means experience influences brain development. A clear illustration of this point comes from the warning of physicians: Never, ever cover the eye of an infant or toddler with a bandage. Why? Input from the eyes is essential for the normal development of the brain's visual cortex. If one

eye is covered, the eye will develop normally, but the connections it makes with visual neurons in the brain will not. A child can become not "eye-blind" but "brain-blind," a currently untreatable condition.

J. Madeleine Nash writes, "Of all the discoveries that have poured out of neuroscience labs in recent years, the finding that the electrical activity of the brain changes the physical structure of the brain is perhaps the most breathtaking. For the rhythmic firing of neurons is no longer assumed to be a by-product of building the brain but essential to the process. . . ."[1]

That means that every experience you have from birth to the grave changes how your neurons interact. Positive learning experiences strengthen desirable neuronal connections. Negative experiences can have disastrous consequences both for brain and for behavior. For example, isolation is known to cause aggressive behavior in both humans and other animals. French scientists have found that isolation reduces the levels of serotonin and GABA in the brains of rats. These neurotransmitters are inhibitors of aggressive behavior.

Another study conducted at the University of Massachusetts tells a chilling tale full of lessons for human beings. In nature, hamsters live alone after they leave their mothers at about three weeks old. Scientists experimented by taking young hamsters and putting them in cages with older ones. That caused trouble. The older animals threatened and sometimes attacked the newcomers.

The younger animals were then put in cages of their own, and other hamsters were brought in. If the visitors were their same size, the hamsters tried to hide or run away. But when confronted with a younger or weaker intruder, they attacked—much more viciously than they themselves had been attacked.

"These hamsters became far more aggressive than normal," says scientist Craig Ferris. Measurements of the hamsters' brain chemistry gave clues about why. Animals who had experienced violence early in life were more sensitive to vasopressin, a brain chemical associated with aggression. The neural pathways that let serotonin control aggression were also abnormal.

Ferris believes that the same thing happens in people. Youngsters who grow up in a violent environment become violent themselves. The time to stop this cycle, he says, is early in childhood.

If Neurons Specialize, How Does My Brain Give Me an Organized View of the World?

June Kinoshita asks the question this way: "Playing middle C on a piano stimulates neurons that variously detect the edges of the key, whiteness, 264-hertz vibrations, and fingertip pressure. The brain fragments the world into atoms of experience. Why, then, do we experience it as one?"[2]

Brain scientists disagree on the answer to that question. Maybe the visual neurons that detect the edge of the key and its whiteness pass along their information to "higher level" cells that relate sight to touch. Still other neurons might add sound to the mixture, and so on, until a complete comprehension of the playing of middle C is created. Such an "association cortex," some believe, would store what Kinoshita calls the "complete essence of an experience, something like a finished movie." One problem with this explanation is that it seems to require a separate "movie" for every experience. That's more memory capacity than anybody has.

So maybe the brain doesn't store separate facts or groups of facts. Perhaps, instead, it's not the destination that counts but the journey. Imagine circuits of neurons as highways that facts travel along. Hearing middle C played on the piano starts signals speeding along a route linking memories just as roads connect towns. At some intersection, the separate roads traveled by perceptions of the key's touch, and its sound and appearance, all come together into the unique combination of sensations you associate with playing middle C.

Like a highway network, perhaps brain networks allow side trips, detours, and alternate routes. Signals taking different paths—then meeting again at some other crossroads—might describe how the brain relates middle C to the honk of a goose, the toot of a horn, the range of a baritone, or the drone of a car's engine. It also suggests how composers can use the eight notes of the scale to create everything from Bach to heavy metal.

Unfortunately, the highway comparison is just a way of thinking about how the brain might work. The idea that knowledge is distributed widely around the brain is now generally accepted. But how the brain indexes and cross-references that knowledge remains a mystery.

Are There Really Only Five Senses?

We usually talk about the five senses: vision, hearing, taste, touch, and smell. Actually, it's seven if we include temperature and pain as separate from touch. These are the senses you are conscious of, but there are others you scarcely notice. Think about these experiences:

- You fall into a swimming pool. Somehow you know which way to swim to reach the surface.

- You close your eyes and spin around. You may teeter, but you don't fall down.

- You do a double flip off the high bar in gymnastics. Without thinking, you "know" where your body is in the air and how to land on two feet.

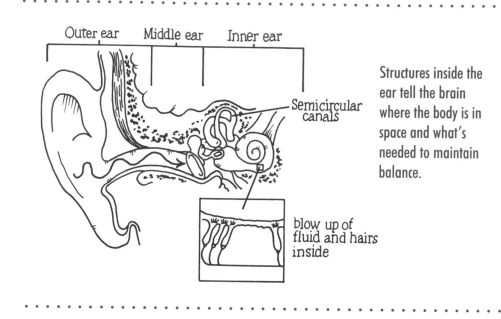

Outer ear Middle ear Inner ear

Semicircular
canals

Structures inside the
ear tell the brain
where the body is in
space and what's
needed to maintain
balance.

blow up of
fluid and hairs
inside

Your brain senses the position of your body in space. Without consciously thinking about it, you know up from down. Your brain "knows" if your muscles are relaxed or contracted, and it is constantly receiving information on the angle of your joints, the tilt of your head. Your brain automatically adjusts your muscles and bones, ligaments and tendons, so you stand or sit without falling (unless an icy sidewalk or a broken chair tricks your brain).

Your brain gets the information it needs to keep you balanced from structures in your inner ear. Two sacs there contain tiny crystals, or stones, that let the brain know the body's position in relation to the pull of gravity. Also important are the semicircular canals. When you move your head, fluid inside the canals changes position. That causes some tiny hairlike projections inside the canals to move. Their movement stimulates neurons that send messages to the cerebellum, brain stem, and spinal cord.

What happens when you become dizzy? If you've been spinning for a while, the fluid in the canals keeps whirling after you have stopped. Movement of the fluid is what causes seasickness, too.

You have lots of other senses, too, although you aren't aware of them. For example:

- Your brain detects the levels of sugar and salt in your blood. If levels are low, feelings of hunger and thirst are the result.

- Pressure receptors in the walls of the heart and large blood vessels pick up changes in blood pressure. The brain responds by sending a message to the heart to beat faster or slower.

- Your brain can detect changes in body temperature. Get caught out in the cold and you'll find yourself shivering. That's one of nature's best involuntary warm-up exercises.

What Parts of My Brain Allow Me to Talk?

The search for an answer to that question began in 1837. Marc Dax, a French country doctor, presented a paper to a medical society in Montpelier. He had noticed that some of his patients who had lost the ability to speak had damage to the left sides of their brains. Dax suggested that language might be controlled by the left hemisphere. Nobody paid much attention to Dax's idea, partly because any suggestion of localization of brain function smacked of phrenology, and phrenology was a laughing matter in scientific circles.

By 1864 they weren't laughing anymore. That year, French surgeon Pierre Paul Broca proclaimed with confidence, "We speak with the left

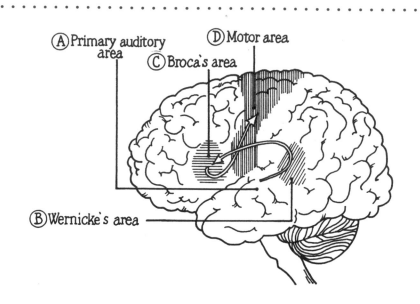

How speech is routed through the brain. A) The primary auditory cortex hears the word. B) Wernicke's area structures the signal. C) The impulse travels from Wernicke's area to Broca's area via the arcuate fasciculus. D) The motor area receives the impulse and directs the lips, teeth, tongue, and palate to form the word.

side of our brain!" He came to that conclusion after performing autopsies on people who had speech disorders, among them his most famous patient, "Tan." Tan understood what people said to him, but he could neither speak nor write words of his own. The only word he could say was "Tan."

After Tan died, Broca did an autopsy. He found a piece as big as a hen's egg missing from Tan's left frontal lobe. After studying the brains of fifteen patients like Tan, Broca suggested that the damaged area might be the brain's speech center. In that part of the left hemisphere, thoughts take the form of speech. Broca's area (named in honor of its discoverer) lies close to the parts of the brain that control movement of the tongue, lips, palate, and vocal cords.

About a decade later, a German doctor, Karl Wernicke, studied people with a different problem. They could speak, but their words were nonsense, and they had trouble understanding what was said to them. Wernicke found damage in a different area of the left temporal lobe, now called Wernicke's area. That's where language is decoded for meaning and where logical speech is put together.

For normal speech, Wernicke's and Broca's areas must communicate. When they can't, the person may be able to understand words—even think clearly—but speak only gibberish. However, Broca's area can work alone. That happens when we simply parrot back what we hear without thinking about its meaning.

Of course, these language centers must communicate with other areas of the brain to produce ideas worth talking about. For example, neurons in the visual cortex register the perception that we think of as color. To see red, to think red, and then to say "red" requires the coordinated action of many different parts of the brain.

Is Sign Language Different From Spoken Language?

Not in any fundamental way. Sign language uses movement and vision instead of sound as input for the speech centers of the left hemisphere. The brain can make the substitution rather easily, especially if sign language is learned when very young. Stroke victims who lose the ability to name objects can sometimes recall words they have forgotten by learning their signs.

Incidentally, no matter how many different languages you learn, they're all stored in the same part of the brain.

It depends. Although reading out loud uses the brain's speech centers, reading words and hearing them aren't the same. Areas in the back of the brain process words in print, while centers in the temporal lobes perceive spoken words. PET pictures can show the difference. In one experiment, right-handed people read a list of nouns aloud. Their brains showed increased activity in five areas of the left occipital lobe. When the subjects heard those same nouns said aloud, those areas remained inactive.

If you read a word aloud, a signal from the visual cortex travels to the angular gyrus, which triggers Wernicke's area. The rest of the process is the same as in the previous illustration.

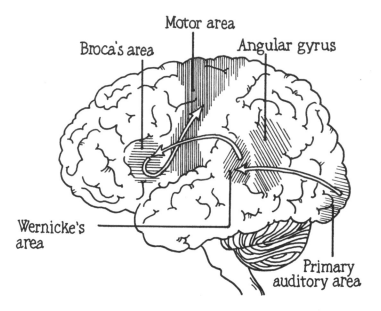

Motor area

Broca's area

Angular gyrus

Wernicke's area

Primary auditory area

Reading out loud is different from silent reading. To speak as you read, information sent from the eyes to the visual cortex must travel to another of the brain's speech centers, the angular gyrus. There, the look of the word is matched with the correct sound pattern in Wernicke's area. Signals then activate neurons in Broca's area to make the mouth, tongue, and vocal cords produce the correct sounds.

When reading silently, you don't need either Wernicke's area or the angular gyrus to understand the meaning of a written word, at least not one you already know. You may need to "sound out" new words, but those you have already learned can be decoded by the brain's visual centers alone.

Does Practice Make My Brain Perfect?

Maybe not perfect, but it does change the areas of the brain that work at a specific task. For example, some scientists asked volunteers to suggest a verb to go with a noun. Some examples are "apple-eat" or "mouse-run." They took PET pictures of the volunteers' brains when they first started the task and later, after fifteen minutes of practice. They found that, while the matching required a lot of brainwork at first, after practice it had become as easy as reading out loud.

What Causes Speech Problems Such as Stuttering?

Stuttering is only one of dozens of problems of speech and language. Each is different in its symptoms and, probably, its cause.

Although about one child in four will stutter between the ages of two and seven, 80 percent stop before they reach adulthood.[3] More than three million Americans, half of whom are young children, stutter.[4] Stuttering affects four times as many males as females.[5]

Although not the same for everyone, stuttering often involves one or more of the following:

- repeating whole words (He . . . He . . . He . . . went)
- repeating parts of words (f-f-f-father or fa-fa-fa-father)
- extending certain sounds for more than a second (hhhhouse or ssssister)
- long breaks between syllables (bro . . . ther)
- jerky sentences
- physically straining to speak (for example, blinking, grimacing, pursing the lips, or clenching the fists)
- opening the mouth without any sound coming out

Stuttering has long been explained as a psychological or emotional problem. Some say that children will stutter if parents are too demanding or the environment is threatening. William H. Perkins of the University of Southern California's Stuttering Center blames conflict for the problem. The child stutters to get attention from his parents, Perkins says.

New research findings challenge such explanations. Some speech experts think that stuttering may be a fault of hearing. If we can't hear ourselves correctly, we can't speak correctly.

Others think that a fault in the brain's language-processing centers may be to blame. Researchers at the University of California, Irvine took PET pictures of the brains of stutterers. They found low brain activity in the left caudate nucleus, a structure deep in the brain's core. It works like a switchboard, connecting thoughts with words. The caudate is connected to the limbic system, the seat of emotions. Maybe that explains why stress makes stuttering worse.

Gerald Maguire, one of the scientists working on the project and himself a stutterer, believes that drugs that block the neurotransmitter dopamine may help stutterers. Other researchers are experimenting with antidepressant and anti-anxiety drugs. But drugs can't replace speech therapy, Maguire says.

Stutterers are sometimes considered stupid or are rejected by other people. They may get so self-conscious about their stuttering that they avoid going out or applying for jobs. But stuttering needn't hold a person back. Winston Churchill, Marilyn Monroe, Carly Simon, Bruce Willis, and James Earl Jones are just a few of the famous people who overcame stuttering.

If you have a friend who stutters, take this advice:

- The person who is speaking deserves attention and respect.
- Communication is easier for everyone in a relaxed, unhurried environment.
- Be polite. Don't interrupt or finish words or sentences. Telling a stutterer to "slow down" is no help.

What Causes Reading Disabilities Such as Dyslexia?

Dyslexia is a learning disability in which letters and numbers are jumbled. That causes problems in mastering reading, writing, and arithmetic. Dyslexics commonly read words backwards, mix up letters such as *b* and *d*, read upside down, or even write from right to left with either hand. A dyslexic's eyes may see "bog," but the hand writes "gob." The order of numbers can cause problems, too; dyslexics may confuse amounts of money, addresses, or telephone numbers. As many as 15 percent of Americans may have learning problems associated with dyslexia.[6]

Dyslexia seems to run in families, so some researchers are looking for a genetic connection. More boys are dyslexic than girls, so maybe hormones have something to do with it. Because dyslexia shows up more often in babies born in summer, some researchers think a winter flu virus might infect pregnant women and interfere with brain development before birth.

Other studies claim that dyslexia results from a failure of one hemisphere to take charge over the other. If both left and right hemispheres compete to control reading and writing, confusion and errors could result. Magnetic resonance and PET images have offered more clues. The thalamus, which relays sensory information to the cortex, is less active in poor readers, researchers at Wake Forest University found. Also, dyslexics seem to have less activity in a part of the right hemisphere known to process language.

The problem may lie in processing what the eyes see, but a defect in handling what the ear hears may be the culprit, too. For example, the left hemispheres of dyslexic children seem to be missing some cells that specialize in understanding rapid sounds in speech. (Consonants such as b, d, and g are rapid; m and n are slow.) The area of the thalamus that processes sound impulses and passes them on to the cortex is smaller in the left hemisphere of dyslexics.

Because dyslexics make mistakes with spelling and numbers, they may be laughed at or labeled stupid, when, in truth, just the opposite is true. Most dyslexics are of average or above-average intelligence. Help for dyslexia lies not in ridicule but in acceptance, understanding, and respect.

Dyslexics can and do overcome their learning problems. Special techniques for teaching reading can work wonders, as can strategies for decreasing distraction and anxiety. The list of famous people who have found ways around their dyslexia includes Cher, Tom Cruise, Henry Winkler, Whoopi Goldberg, and Greg Louganis.

Is It True that Most People Use Only a Tiny Fraction of Their Brainpower?

Maybe we could all benefit from using our heads a bit more, but no scientific evidence supports the claim that we could all be Einsteins if we worked at it. Actually, PET scans show that the brains of people who score high on intelligence tests don't "work as hard" (use as much oxygen and sugar) as those of their average-scoring friends and neighbors.

What's the Difference Between Brain and Mind?

Since the dawn of human self-awareness millions of years ago, we have wondered about ourselves and our place in the universe. Do we exist apart from our bodies? Do we live after our bodies die? Is there meaning to human existence? Do purpose, order, and immortality exist in a plane of reality beyond what our senses can perceive? Some people believe that the chemistry and physics of the brain explain all that we are. Others think that the essence of our being and the meaning of our lives lie outside what scanners can see and probes can measure.

Is there a difference between the brain (the organ we think with) and the mind (the content of our thoughts)? Neurologist and writer Richard Restak says no: "Mind can affect brain; brain can affect mind. But can either be separated from the other? Not any more than the other side of this paper can be separated from the side you are now reading," he wrote.[7]

Francis Crick, a Nobel Prize-winner for his work on DNA, shares Restak's view. In his book, *The Astonishing Hypothesis*, he writes: "'You, your joys and your sorrows, your memories and your ambitions, your sense of personal identity and free will, are in fact no more than the behavior of a vast assembly of nerve cells and their associated molecules."[8] He calls the brain a machine that only believes itself to have free will. "Free will," he says, "is located at or near the anterior cingulate sulcus."[9]

Candace Pert, discoverer of morphine receptors in the brain, takes a broader but equally mechanical view. She believes that the mind is the interaction between the brain and a cocktail of neurotransmitters made—and operating—at various sites around the body. She says that sinking feeling in the pit of your stomach when you fall in love is simply a chemical process—nothing more than the docking of proteins in their receptor sites. Is love the same for everybody? Absolutely, according to Pert.

In one form or another, the views expressed by Restak, Crick, and Pert have been around at least since the fourth century B.C. when Hippocrates, the "Father of Medicine," wrote:

From the brain, and from the brain alone, arise our pleasures, joys, laughter, and jests, as well as our sorrows, pains, griefs, and fears. Through it, in particular, we think, see, hear, and distinguish the ugly from the beautiful, the bad from the good. . . .

Objections to this view of people as machines go back centuries, too. Immanuel Kant, an eighteenth-century German philosopher, was one among many to reject the mechanical view of mind and brain as one. "No experience tells me that I am shut up some place in my brain," he wrote.[10] Nobel Prize-winning neuroscientist C.S. Sherrington agreed. He wrote of mind and brain: "That our being should consist of two fundamental elements offers, I suppose, no greater inherent improbability than that it should rest on the one only."[11]

In this view, consciousness is something special, indefinable, spiritual. The brain is a physical organ, but its products—thoughts, feelings, dreams and aspirations—have a life of their own unconfined by time, space, or the laws of the universe. Nobel Prize-winning brain scientist Sir John Eccles felt comfortable with that idea:

> I go all the way with my fellow scientists in understanding the brain physically. But it doesn't explain me, or human choice, delight, courage, or compassion. I believe we must go beyond. So I'm a heretic, a dualist who firmly believes that there is something apart from all the electricity and chemistry we can measure. I think there is more wonder and mystery than we realize."[12]

In the end, each of us must decide. Are we mystery or machine, miracle or matter? David Gelman summed up the dilemma this way: "Is the mind an illusion? Yes, say the philosopher-scientists. The brain is a machine. How do they know? Well, it's just a matter of faith."[13]

The Bard and the Brain

· · · · ·

Here is more matter for a hot brain.

WILLIAM SHAKESPEARE

(THE WINTER'S TALE)

· · · · ·

What does a sixteenth-century playwright have to do with that "three-pound universe" inside your skull? A lot, if you start to examine the thoughts about the brain expressed by (some say) the greatest of all English-speaking writers.

Imagine yourself back in 1592. That year, Shakespeare completed the second part of his epic saga *King Henry VI*. The play tells of a plot to take over the throne of England. In the third act, York, intent on grabbing the crown for himself, describes his planning for war: "My brain more busy than a laboring spider weaves tedious snares to trap mine enemies," he says.

Shakespeare, it seems, had ideas about the workings of the human brain, regardless of the state of scientific knowledge at the time. The ancient Greek physician Hippocrates considered the brain the "organ of the mind and the temple of the soul." The philosopher Plato agreed, but Aristotle, Plato's student, had other ideas. He called the heart the body's nerve center and the source of all thoughts. The brain, he said, was a radiator for cooling the blood.

Shakespeare often showed the head and the heart at odds with each other. "The brain may devise laws for the blood," Shakespeare writes in *The Merchant of Venice*, "but a hot temper leaps o'er a cold decree." So much for thinking twice and counting to ten.

No conflict of head and heart was more problematic for Shakespeare than love (sometimes called "fancy" in Shakespeare's time). "Tell me where is fancy bred . . . in the heart or in the head?" he asks in *The Merchant of Venice*. Though his comedies come down on the side of the heart most of the time, he gives the brain its fair share of romantic action. In *Much Ado About Nothing*, Benedick's love for Beatrice is revealed after friends produce "a paper written in his hand, a halting sonnet of his own pure brain." (Beatrice's brain had been similarly engaged, it appears, for she wrote a love poem, too.)

Still, Shakespeare can't see love as a matter of mind alone. Love's too grand to be confined to the brain, he argues in *Love's Labour's Lost*:

But love, first learned in a lady's eyes,
Lives not alone immured in the brain;
But, with the motion of all elements,
Courses as swift as thought in every
*   power,*

And gives to every power a double
*   power,*
Above their functions and their
*   offices.*

The ancients invented so-called humors to explain how mind and body might work. Four fluids— phlegm, blood, yellow bile, and black bile—were thought to make people sick or well. Shakespeare seems to have accepted that idea. For example, he describes the Duke in *As You Like It* as "humorous"—not meaning funny but in a foul temper.

Scientists and physicians of medieval times thought that three "spirits" controlled the body. The liver made natural spirit with food from the intestines. Natural spirit traveled to the heart where it changed into vital spirit. Vital spirit then went to the brain where it mixed with air from the lungs to form the life force or animal spirit. Medieval sketches show the ventricles or cavities of the brain as reservoirs for animal spirit. From there, it flowed to all parts of the body through the nerves, which were thought to be hollow tubes. Shakespeare had no reason to dispute such theories. Indeed, he embraced them warmly, speaking often (as he did in *Twelfth Night*) of liver, brain, and heart as "sovereign thrones."

Shakespeare would be dead nearly fifty years before the English physician Thomas Willis would publish his landmark book *Cerebri anatome*. In it, he would show the arrangement of nerves in the head and correctly identify the cerebrum as the seat of thought. Ahead of his time, Shakespeare portrayed learning and memory as products of the brain. For example, to the ghost of his father the king, Hamlet vows to forget all that he knows and seek vengeance against his father's killer:

Yea, from the table of my memory
I'll wipe away all trivial fond
*   records,*
All saws of books, all forms, all
*   pressures past,*
That youth and observation copied
*   there;*
And thy commandment all alone
*   shall live*
Within the book and volume of my
*   brain . . .*

Shakespeare thought that romance and insanity had a lot in common (and he found both far more interesting than normality). He wrote in *A Midsummer Night's Dream*, "Lovers and madmen have such seething brains, such shaping fantasies, that apprehend more than cool reason ever comprehends."

The bard especially liked mental deviations. Quite a few of his characters were mad, demented, or (in his words) "brainsick." "What madness rules in brainsick men?" asks King Henry VI, weary of major battles over minor disagreements. Later, as Henry's tale continues, Shakespeare labels Eleanor (an enemy of the king) "a bedlam brain-sick duchess."

Perhaps the most memorable of all Shakespeare's crazed characters is Lady Macbeth, who drives her husband to murder the King of Scotland. After the murder, she is so deranged by guilt that her husband pleads with a doctor to give her some medicine to make her forget:

Cure her of that,
Canst thou not minister to a mind
*   diseased,*
Pluck from the memory a rooted
*   sorrow,*
Raze out the written troubles of the
*   brain*

And with some sweet oblivious
        antidote
Cleanse the stuff'd bosom of that
        perilous stuff
Which weighs upon the heart?

(The doctor can work no such magic. Lady Macbeth commits suicide. Read the play to find out Macbeth's fate.)

Shakespeare is at his funniest and best when he hurls insults at brains. He calls one brain "as dry as a remainder biscuit after a voyage." He accuses his characters of having "no more brain than a stone," and "no more brain . . . than in mine elbows." In *Troilus and Cressida*, Thersites gives Agamemnon credit for being honest and loving quails, but "he has not so much brain as earwax."

For all the fun, the brain was a serious matter to the bard. The organ, "which some suppose the soul's frail dwelling-house," *(King John),* figured prominently in Shakespeare's plays. Shakespeare saw the brain as too serious a matter to be left to science. To him, it was literature, art, the source of human expression. Perhaps Shakespeare saw the brain in two ways: as the doorway to the universe and the only universe a human being can inhabit. In Shakespeare's words, there is "nowhere else but in your brain."

IN CLOSING:
MORE QUESTIONS THAN ANSWERS

In the human head there are forces within forces within forces,
as in no other cubic half-foot of the universe that we know.

• ROGER SPERRY •

What have you thought about as you've read the questions and answers on these pages? Perhaps you have been struck by how complex the brain is. All those neurons, networks, impulses, neurotransmitters. On and on the maze of connections and interactions goes. How can anyone possibly understand it all? The truth is, no one does, and some people question whether anyone ever will. This marvelous organ that composes symphonies, builds skyscrapers, and explores space may have found its limit—in trying to understand itself.

Did you notice, also, that every answer only raised more questions? No matter how far we have come in explaining how neurons send and receive signals, we're not much nearer now than we ever were to knowing how those signals translate into thoughts, senses, feelings, or action. Still as much a mystery as ever is that three pounds of mush that lets its owner catch a fish, sing an aria, bake a cake, write a poem . . . or wonder about itself.

Perhaps also you began to develop some sense of your place in history. Brain science today is like geography in the Age of Discovery when explorers first landed on the shores of continents.[1] Today's explorers of the human brain can see the edges of things and suspect there is something vast beyond—but what? Like pioneers braving new frontiers, scientists invite all of us to set off into uncharted territory. Also like pioneers of the past, we are plagued by mixed feelings. We may be excited by the prospects of discovery, but at the same time afraid of what lies ahead. After all, the brain that explores itself may not like what it uncovers.

Finally, you may have looked ahead to ask how the human brain will use its new understanding of itself. Will brain science enhance our humanity or undermine it? Will probing the secrets of the organ that shapes us, drives us, and defines us make us more human—or less so? The answer will come from brains like yours and mine and from the brains of our children and grandchildren. How will we and generations to come respond to the conquest of our last and innermost frontier? Look for that answer inside yourself, inside that brain of yours. That's where more questions than answers lie, and asking questions is what healthy brains do best.

Table 1
SOME PARTS OF THE BRAIN AND THEIR FUNCTIONS

PART	FUNCTION
Amygdala	Part of the limbic system involved in forming memories.
Angular gyrus	An area through which speech impulses travel.
Arcuate fasciculus	An area through which speech impulses travel.
Auditory cortex	An area in the temporal lobe of the cerebrum responsible for hearing.
Blood-brain barrier	Dense network of cells in tightly packed blood vessels that prevents large molecules, including many poisons, from entering the brain.
Brain stem	The "reptilian brain" that controls basic functions such as breathing and heart beat.
Broca's area	Speech center that directs the physical production of speech sounds.
Caudate nucleus	An area that connects thoughts and words. Also important in movement.
Cerebellum	Controls coordination, posture, balance, and some learned physical skills.
Cerebrospinal fluid	Fluid in the brain ventricles and backbone that protects the brain and spinal cord.
Cerebrum/cerebral cortex	"New mammalian" or "thinking" brain controls thought, purpose, personality.
Corpus callosum	The bundle of 300 million nerve fibers that connects the right and left hemispheres.
Glial cells	Support neurons in the brain.Thought to mop up neurotransmitters at the synaptic gap and to control speed of neural firing.

PART	FUNCTION
Hippocampus	Part of the limbic system involved in forming memories.
Hypothalamus	Part of the brain that controls the pituitary. Monitors temperature, hunger, thirst.
Limbic system	"Old mammalian brain" governs basic functions and emotions.
Locus coeruleus	One of the brain's sleep-wake centers.
Meninges	Layers of tissue inside the skull that protect the brain.
Motor cortex	A strip of the cerebral cortex responsible for voluntary movements.
Neurons	Nerve cells that carry Impulses to, from, and within the brain.
Pituitary gland	The body's master gland responsible for manufacturing several different hormones that affect growth, reproduction, and vital life processes.
Reticular formation	Neurons in the brain stem responsible for alertness and concentration.
Thalamus	The brain's "switchboard" that filters sensory data to be sent to the cortex.
Ventricles	Cavities in the brain filled with cerebrospinal fluid.
Visual cortex	Part of the occipital lobe of the cerebrum that handles vision.
Wernicke's area	Center where language is decoded for meaning and logical speech is constructed.

Table 2
SOME NEUROTRANSMITTERS AND THEIR FUNCTIONS

NEUROTRANSMITTER	FUNCTION	NOTES
Acetylcholine	In muscles, causes contraction. In brain, appears necessary for normal intellectual function. Plays a role in memory.	Acetylcholine levels are low in people with Alzheimer's disease.
Dopamine	Three circuits: 1. Regulates glands that produce hormones. 2. Regulates movement. 3. Involved in emotions and learning.	1. Directs the hypothalamus to manufacture hormones and triggers the release of hormones from the pituitary gland. 2. The brains of people with Parkinson's disease have hardly any dopamine. 3. Drugs that keep dopamine from attaching to receptors in the brain relieve symptoms in some schizophrenics.
Epinephrine and norepinephrine	Epinephrine is secreted by the adrenal gland in response to stress. It increases blood pressure and heart rate, preparing the body for action. In the brain, norepinephrine is more prevalent. It may be important to memory and learning.	Norepinephrine levels are low in the brains of people with Alzheimer's disease. May also play a role in depression.
GABA (gamma-aminobutyric acid)	A major inhibitor. Prevents action in various brain centers.	The prefrontal cortex of schizophrenics may lack the ability to make enough GABA.
Glutamate and aspartate (amino acids)	Promote the firing of neurons. May be associated with learning, memory, and the development of nerve connections.	Too much stimulation may cause cell death and stroke.
Hormones	Glands release hormones into the blood that, in turn, stimulate other organs to release still other hormones. These mechanisms regulate everything from metabolism (getting energy from food) to emotion, responses to stress, and sexual behavior.	Some scientists do not consider hormones neurotransmitters.

NEUROTRANMITTER	FUNCTION	NOTES
Neurotrophic factors	Affect the growth, nature, and survival of neurons during development.	Research on neurotrophic factors may lead to promising new treatments for brain disorders.
Opioids, including enkephalin and other endorphins	Reduce pain. Cause sleepiness.	Named because of their opium-like action. Enkephalin and the other endorphins act like morphine.
Serotonin	Causes blood vessels to constrict. Influences moods. Important to sleeping and waking. Serotonin receptors (maybe 20 different kinds) are found in many parts of the body, not just the brain.	Imbalances can cause anxiety, depression, addiction, schizophrenia, migraine headaches, and nausea. Prozac, a drug used to treat depression, increases levels of serotonin in the brain by slowing the removal of serotonin from the synapses.

Table 3
HOW SOME ADDICTIVE DRUGS ARE THOUGHT TO WORK

DRUG	NEUROTRANSMITTER INTERFERENCE
Alcohol	May bind to metenkephalin sites producing (initially) feelings of well-being and (later) metenkephalin deficiency. May lower brain levels of GABA and serotonin. An older theory is that alcohol alters the electrical excitability of nerve cell membranes.
Amphetamines (speed)	Cause dopamine and norepinephrine to leak into synapse and interfere with their re-uptake. The combined effect is increased stimulation of receptors.
Barbiturates (examples include Seconal, Phenobarbital, and Valium)	May increase the inhibitory effects of GABA.
Cocaine and crack (a chemically altered form of cocaine)	Interfere with the process by which dopamine and serotonin are reabsorbed by the neuron that produced them. A decrease in dopamine leads to a craving for more cocaine.
Hallucinogens: marijuana, mescaline, and LSD (lysergic acid diethylamide)	The active ingredient in marijuana, THC, affects the electrical properties of nerve membranes and affects the turnover rates of serotonin and dopamine. LSD blocks serotonin receptors.
Heroin and morphine (opiate drugs derived from the opium poppy)	Inhibits the release of the neurotransmitter, substance P, thereby dulling the pain messages. Also attaches to receptors in pleasure centers and breathing centers of the brain.
Nicotine	Attaches to acetylcholine receptors. First stimulates, then blocks, incoming impulses.

EFFECTS

In low doses, a stimulant; in higher doses, a depressant. Reduces anxiety, tension, and inhibitions. Impairs muscle control, delays reaction time, clouds thinking. Stimulates appetite, causes loss of body heat and water.

A stimulant. Dilates bronchial tubes in the lungs. Blocks sleep. Depresses appetite.

"Downers." Tranquilizers. Sleep inducers.

Temporary feelings of euphoria, power, and self-confidence. Blood vessels constrict and the normal heart rhythm is disrupted. After a "binge," depression, drowsiness, lethargy, loss of appetite.

Distort the senses and perception of reality; can produce delusions, hallucinations, severe anxiety, and psychosis in some people.

A rush of euphoria followed by a relaxed state. In small doses, relieves pain, slows breathing, stops diarrhea, but can cause nausea and vomiting. In larger doses, can stop breathing, causing death.

Constricts blood vessels near the skin. Lowers skin temperature. Increases blood pressure and metabolic rate (speed at which food is burned for energy). Decreases oxygen-carrying ability of blood, causing shortness of breath.

NOTES

Consumption of alcohol by pregnant women causes fetal alcohol syndrome, the leading cause of preventable mental retardation. Chronic liver disease caused by alcohol consumption kills 25,000 Americans every year.

Can cause hallucinations and paranoia.

Interfere with learning and memory. Life-threatening if taken in large doses or with alcohol.

Cocaine binds to heart cells as well as brain cells, damaging the heart muscle.

Alcohol, tobacco, and marijuana are often considered "gateway" drugs as their use in early life may lead to cocaine and heroin use later.

Addicts experience painful withdrawal symptoms including muscle pain, cramps, and diarrhea. Drugs such as nalorphine, naloxone, and naltrexone block opiate effects. Methadone is used in some treatment programs to control craving, withdrawal symptoms, and relapse.

Increases risk of death from many forms of cancer, respiratory diseases, and heart disease. Reduces years of life.

NOTES

Chapter One

1. A lower estimate of 10-100 billion neurons appears in Judith Hooper and Dick Teresi, *The Three-Pound Universe* (Los Angeles: Jeremy P. Tarcher, Inc., 1986), p. 30; also in Bennett Daviss, "Brain Powered," *Discover* (May 1994), p. 62. A higher estimate of 300 billion appears in Richard Restak, *The Brain Has a Mind of Its Own: Insights From a Practicing Neurologist* (New York: Crown, 1991). Most other books use the 100 billion estimate. The number of glial cells may be as much as ten times greater than the number of neurons.
2. J. Madeleine Nash, "The Frontier Within," *Time* (Fall 1992), p. 82.
3. Jack Fincher, *The Brain: Mystery of Matter and Mind* (Washington, DC: U.S. News Books, 1981).
4. The Diagram Group, *The Brain: A User's Manual* (New York: Perigee Books, 1982), p. 108.
5. Ibid., p. 19.
6. Hooper and Teresi, *The Three-Pound Universe*, p. 36.
7. Diane Connors, "Interview: Michael Gazzaniga," *Omni* (October 1993), pp. 99-100.
8. *How Things Work: The Brain* (Alexandria, VA: Time-Life Books, 1990), p. 8.
9. Joel Swerdlow, "Quiet Miracles of the Brain," *National Geographic* (June 1995), p. 10.

10. *How Things Work: The Brain*, pp. 9-10.
11. Madeleine J. Nash, "Fertile Minds," *Time* (February 3, 1997).
12. Ibid.
13. Marcia Baringa, "How the Brain Weeds Its Garden," *Science* (March 4, 1994), p. 1225.
14. For more on this idea, see Daniel Golden, "Building a Better Brain," *Life* (July 1994), pp. 62-70.
15. Richard Restak, *The Brain Has a Mind of Its Own*, p. 141.
16. Robert Ornstein and Richard F. Thompson, *The Amazing Brain* (Boston: Houghton Mifflin, 1984), p. 168.
17. Marc McCutcheon, *The Compass in Your Nose and Other Astonishing Facts About Humans* (Los Angeles: Jeremy P. Tarcher, 1989), p. 68.
18. Jack Fincher, *The Brain: Mystery of Matter and Mind*, p. 123.
19. Ibid.
20. Quoted in Polly Shulman, "Snooze Button," *Discover* (January 1997)
21. How do scientists see brain cells at work? See "Imaging the Brain," p. 42.
22. Susan Greenfield, "The Electric Ape," The Royal Institution of Great Britain Christmas Lectures, 1994, London: BBC Television.
23. Margery and Howard Facklam, *The Brain: Magnificent Mind Machine* (San Diego: Harcourt Brace Jovanovich, 1982), p. 15.
24. Quoted in Bruce Schechter, "Ports of Recall: The Neurolink," *Omni* (April 1988), pp. 65-66.
25. Kathy A. Fackelmann, "Anatomy of Alzheimer's," *Science News* (December 5, 1992), p. 394.
26. Schecter, "Ports of Recall," *Omni* (April 1988), pp. 65-66.
27. Quoted in George Howe Holt, "The Power of Dreams," *Life* (September 1995), p. 42.

Chapter Two

1. Ornstein and Thompson, p. 67.
2. Frank W. Pfrieger and Barbara A. Barres, "Synaptic Efficacy Enhanced by Glial Cells in Vitro," *Science* (September 12, 1997), pp. 1684-86.
3. Richard Restak, *The Brain Has a Mind of Its Own* (New York: Crown Books, 1991), p. 196.
4. Helena Curtis, *Biology* (4th ed.) (New York: Worth, 1983), p. 770.
5. Ibid., p. 771.

6. The Diagram Group, *The Brain: A User's Manual*, p. 41.
7. Hyperion, 1995.
8. Roger Highfield, "Dieting Is All in the Head," *The London Daily Telegraph* (August 17, 1995).
9. Richard Restak, *The Brain Has a Mind of Its Own*, p. 119.
10. "Memories Are Made of This," *The Economist* (September 8, 1990), p. 98.
11. Ornstein and Thompson, *The Amazing Brain*, pp. 68 and 21.
12. Attributed to Gerald Edelman, *Bright Air, Brilliant Fire*, in J. Madeleine Nash, "The Frontier Within," *Time* (Fall 1992), p. 81.
13. Quoted in Bill Dietrich, "Will Computers Replace Us? Mind Can Make Quantum Leaps Machines Can't," *Seattle Times* (April 18, 1995), p. A12.
14. Quoted in Lisa Seachrist, "Mimicking the Brain: Using Computers to Investigate Neurological Disorders," *Science News* (July 22, 1995), p. 62.
15. Robert P. Crease, "Biomedicine in the Age of Imaging," *Science* (July 30, 1993), p. 558.

Chapter Three

1. Quoted in B. Bower, "Stress Hormones Hike Emotional Memories," *Science News* (October 22, 1994), p. 262.
2. Ornstein and Thompson, *The Amazing Brain*, p. 140.
3. Susan Perry, "Mind Over Matter: Memory," *Current Health* (May 1987), p. 23.
4. *How Things Work: The Brain*, p. 112.
5. Susan Perry, "Mind Over Matter: Memory," p. 23.
6. For one family's story, see "My Problem," *Good Housekeeping* (September 1994), p. 30.
7. Minouche Kandel and Eric Kandel, "Flights of Memory," *Discover* (May 1994), pp. 32-38.
8. Steve Rose, "No Way to Treat the Mind," *New Scientist* (April 17, 1993), p. 26.
9. David Concar, "Brain Boosters," *New Scientist* (Feb. 8, 1997), p. 32.
10. Paul McCarthy, "Use It Or Lose It," *Omni* (February 1994), p. 34.
11. Chris Raymond, "Scientists Examining Behavior of a Man Who Lost His Memory Gain New Insights Into the Workings of the Human Mind," *The Chronicle of Higher Education* (September 20, 1989), p. A4.
12. Bruce Schechter, "Ports of Recall: The Neurolink" *Omni* (April 1988), p. 66.

Chapter Four

1. Ricki Lewis, "Gateway to the Brain," *BioScience* (March 1994), p. 133. If laid flat, the blood-brain barrier would cover an area 20 feet by 50 feet (6.1 by 15.3 meters); that's 1,000 square feet (about 93 square meters), or about the size of an average three-bedroom house.
2. See Natalie Angier, "Storming the Wall," *Discover* (May 1990), pp. 67-72. See also Shannon Brownlee, "Blitzing the Defense: Piercing the Brain's Protective Barrier Is Key to Treating Many Serious Neurological Disorders," *U.S. News & World Report* (October 15, 1990), pp. 90-92.
3. *Brain Concepts: Drugs and the Brain,* pamphlet (Washington, DC: Society for Neuroscience, 1992), p. 1.
4. Associated Press, "Researchers Discover Feel-Good Spot for Nicotine," *The New York Times* (September 23, 1995), p. A11.
5. Phyllis A Feuerstein, "Exercise—or How the Other Half Lives," *Current Health* (March 1987), p. 11.
6. Glenda Cooper, "I Wish That My Child Could Feel Pain," *Independent* (March 24, 1997), p. 15.
7. *How Things Work: The Brain* (Time-Life Books, 1990), p. 99.
8. Quoted in Darryl S. Inaba and William E. Cohen, *Uppers, Downers, All Arounders* (Ashland, OR: Cinemed, 1990), p. 59.
9. Ibid., p. 73.

Chapter Five

1. Sandra Blakeslee, "Old Accident Points to Brain's Moral Center," *The New York Times*, May 24, 1994, p. C1.
2. Alison Mack, "Researchers Link Gene to Epileptic Seizures," *Dallas Morning News* (July 24, 1995), p. 7D.
3. Steven Lewis, "Understanding Epilepsy," *Current Health* (December 1993), p. 21.
4. Ibid.
5. Lisa M. Krieger, "New Drugs to Fight Effects of Stroke Require Prompt Action," *San Francisco Examiner* (August 17, 1995).
6. Gary Taubes, "Will New Dopamine Receptors Offer a Key to Schizophrenia?" *Science* (August 19, 1994), p. 1034.
7. Patricia Anstett, "Schizophrenia Fighter Speaks Out Against the Stigma of Her Illness," *Detroit Free Press* (June 21, 1995).
8. Joel Swerdlow, "Quiet Miracles of the Brain," *National Geographic* (June 1995), p. 11.

9. Eliot Marshal, "A Glimpse of an Elusive Quarry," *Science* (May 12, 1995), p. 793.

10. "March Is the Cruellest [*sic*] Month," *Economist* (August 28, 1993), p. 79.

11. Quoted in Tom Siegfried, "Many Faces of Schizophrenia Reveal Flaws in Brain Circuits," *Dallas Morning News* (July 19, 1995), p. 7D.

12. See the feature "Imaging the Brain, p. 44.)

13. Douglas W. Scharr and Michael Mahler, "Parkinson's Disease: Making the Diagnosis, Selecting Drug Therapies," *Geriatrics* (October 1994), p. 14-23.

14. Moussa B. H. Youdim and Peter Riederer, "Understanding Parkinson's Disease," *Scientific American* (January 1997), p. 52.

15. Shannon Brownlee, "Alzheimer's: Is There Hope?" *U.S. News & World Report* (August 12, 1991), p. 40.

16. Saralie Faivelson, "Alzheimer's: Making Progress in This Progressive Dementia," *Medical World News* (September 1993), p. 22.

17. Nancy L. Mace and Peter V. Rabins, *The 36-Hour Day* (Baltimore: The Johns Hopkins University Press, 1991), p. 285.

18. Robert F. Service, "New Alzheimer's Gene Found," *Science* (June 30, 1995), p. 1845.

19. Zaren S. Khachaturian, "Plundered Memories," *The Sciences* (July/August 1997), p. 24.

20. William Styron, "An Interior Pain That Is All But Indescribable," *Newsweek* (April 18, 1994), pp. 52-53.

21. Constance Holden, "Depression: The News Isn't Depressing," *Science* (December 6, 1991), pp. 1450-1452.

22. "Manic-Depressive Illness Widespread," *USA Today: The Magazine of the American Scene* (October, 1994), p. 13.

23. William Styron, op. cit., p. 52.

24. Constance Holden, op. cit., p. 1452, attributed to Yale psychiatrist George Heninger.

25. Bruce Bower, "The Patients' Perspective on ECT," *Science News* (February 2, 1985), p. 74.

26. "An Inside Look at Electroshock," *Science News* (June 11, 1988), p. 382.

27. David Gelman, "The Mystery of Suicide," *Newsweek* (April 18, 1994), p. 48.

28. Ibid.

29. Harry F. Water, "Teenage Suicide: One Act Not to Follow," *Newsweek* (April 18, 1994), p. 49

30. Sandra Arbetter, "Autism: An Isolation Booth," *Current Health* (May 1988) p. 18.

31. Bruce Bower, "Inside the Autistic Brain," *Science News* (September 6, 1986), p. 154.
32. "The Anatomy of Autism," *Life* (August 1988), p. 63.
33. Bruce Bower, "Promising Addition to Autism Treatment," *Science News* (March 14, 1992), p. 164.
34. Oliver Sacks, "A Neurologist's Notebook: An Anthropologist on Mars," *The New Yorker* (December 27, 1993/January 3, 1994), pp. 106-125.
35. Quoted in Richard L. Hill, "Scientists See No Genetic Fix for Society's Ills," *The Oregonian* (February 20, 1995), p. A8. *Emphasis added.*
36. Read the story of one child's journey in "A New Life for Sarah" by Chris Ravashiere Medvescek, *Parents Magazine* (November 1991), pp. 170-174.
37. Joann Ellison Rogers, "Psychosurgery: Damaging the Brain to Save the Mind," *Psychology Today* (March/April 1992), p. 36.
38. Frances Farmer, *Will There Really Be a Morning? An Autobiography by Frances Farmer* (New York: G.P. Putnam's Sons, 1972), p. 124.
39. Ibid., p. 34.
40. William Arnold, *Shadowland* (New York: McGraw-Hill, 1978), p. 12.
41. Eliot S. Valenstein, *Great and Desperate Cures: The Rise and Decline of Psychosurgery and Other Radical Treatments for Mental Illness* (New York: Basic Books, Inc., 1986), p. 212.

Chapter Six

1. Diane Connors, "Interview: Michael Gazzaniga," *Omni* (October 1993), pp. 99-100, gives the lower estimate. The higher figure is from The Diagram Group, *The Brain: A User's Manual*, p. 108.
2. Diane Connors, "Interview: Michael Gazzaniga," *Omni* (October 1993), pp. 99-100.
3. Antonio R. Damasio and Hanna Damasio, "Brain and Language," *Scientific American* (September 1992), p. 92.
4. Quoted in Dianne Hales, "Why Men Can't Find Things—and Other Great Mysteries Solved," *Ladies Home Journal* (July 1994), p. 68.
5. Steve Jones, *The Language of the Genes: Biology, History, and the Evolutionary Future* (London: HarperCollins, 1993), p. 171.
6. "Right Side of Brain Does the Work for Worriers," Press release, Johns Hopkins, Oct. 25, 1997.
7. Frances Rauscher, "Can Music Make Us More Intelligent?" *Billboard* (October 15, 1994), p. 10.

Chapter Seven

1. *Time* (February 3, 1997), p. 48.
2. *The New York Times Magazine* (October 18, 1992), p. 46.
3. Guy Murdoch, "Stuttering," *Consumers' Research Magazine* (February 1994), p. 2.
4. "The Word on Stuttering," *St. Vincent Times* (Winter/1992), pp. 6-7, as cited in Ann M. Swan, "Helping Children Who Stutter: What Teachers Need to Know," *Childhood Education* (Spring 1993), p. 138.
5. Ibid, p. 141.
6. Estimate attributed to the U.S. Department of Health and Human Services, in Susan Brown as told to Arnold Mann, "My Battle With Dyslexia," *Cosmopolitan* (February 1993), p. 114. See also "Famous People Triumph Over Dyslexia," *Current Science* (February 1994), p. 14.
7. Richard Restak, *The Brain Has a Mind of Its Own*, p. 13.
8. Francis Crick, *The Astonishing Hypothesis: The Scientific Search for the Soul* (New York: Simon and Schuster, 1994), p. 3.
9. Ibid, p. 268.
10. Quoted in Jack Fincher, *The Brain: Mystery of Matter and Mind*.
11. Ibid.
12. Quoted in Margery and Howard Facklam, *The Brain: Magnificent Mind Machine*, p. 7.
13. David Gelman, "Is the Mind an Illusion?" *Newsweek* (April 20, 1992), p. 45.

In Closing

1. June Kinoshita, "Mapping the Mind, *The New York Times Magazine* (October 18, 1992), p. 54.

Table 2

Naomi Freundlich, "Racing to Unlock the Secrets of Serotonin," *Business Week* (November 9, 1992), p. 111.

Table 3

Brain Concepts: Drugs and the Brain, pamphlet (Washington, DC: Society for Neuroscience, 1992), p. 2.

FOR FURTHER INFORMATION

ARTICLES

William F. Allman, "The Musical Brain," *U.S. News and World Report* (June 11, 1990), pp. 58-62.

Sharon Begley, "Mapping the Brain," *Newsweek*, (April 20, 1992), pp. 66-70.

Sharon Begley, "Gray Matters," *Newsweek* (March 27, 1995), pp. 48-54.

Randy Blaun, "Brain Food: How to Eat Smart," *Psychology Today* (May/June 1996), pp. 34-43.

Shannon Brownlee, "Alzheimer's: Is There Hope?" *U. S. News & World Report* (August 12, 1991), pp. 40-47.

Geoffrey Cowley and Anne Underwood, "A Little Help from Serotonin," *Newsweek*, (December 29, 1997/January 5, 1998), pp. 78-81.

Raymond Damadian, "The Story of MRI," *Saturday Evening Post* (May/June 1994), pp. 54-57.

Daniel Golden, "Building a Better Brain," *Life* (July 1994), pp. 63-70.

Erica E. Goode and Joannie M. Schrof, "Where Emotions Come From," *U.S. News & World Report,* (June 24, 1991), pp. 54-62.

Zaven S. Khachaturian, "Plundered Memories," *The Sciences* (July/August 1997), pp. 20-25.

Steven Lewis, "Understanding Epilepsy," *Current Health* (December 1993), pp. 19-21.

"Mysteries of the Mind," *Scientific American*, Special Issue 7 (1997).

J. Madeleine Nash, "Fertile Minds," *Time* (February 3, 1997) p. 48.

Madeleine Nash and Alice Park "Medicine: The Mood Molecule Serotonin Drugs Treat Everything from Depression to Overeating, But As We Learned Last Week, Tinkering with the Chemistry of the Brain Can Be Risky," *Time* (Sept. 29, 1997), p. 74.

Jill Neimart, "Opening the Black Box: Brain Chemistry and Mood Swings," *Psychology Today* (May 15, 1997), p. 33.

John Pakkanen, "I Am Joe's Brain Tumor," *Reader's Digest* (August 1990), pp. 79-83.

Joann Ellison Rodgers, "Addiction: A Whole New View," *Psychology Today* (September 1994), p. 32.

Roger W. Sommi, "Drugs in the Brain," *Current Health* (March 1991), pp. 17-19.

Joel L. Swerdlow, "Quiet Miracles of the Brain," *National Geographic* (June 1995), pp. 2-41.

Andrew Watson, "Why Can't a Computer Be More Like a Brain?" *Science* (September 26, 1997), pp. 1934-1936.

Diana Willensky, "Bodyworks: The Brain," *American Health* (December 1993), pp. 78-79.

Moussa B. H. Youdim and Peter Riederer, "Understanding Parkinson's Disease," *Scientific American* (January 1997), pp. 52-59.

BOOKS

Richard E. Cytowic, *The Man Who Tasted Shapes: A Bizarre Medical Mystery Offers Revolutionary Insights into Emotion, Reasoning and Consciousness.* New York: Putnam, 1993.

The Diagram Group, *The Brain: A User's Manual.* New York: Putnam, 1982.

Bruce H. Dobkin, *Brain Matters: Stories of a Neurologist and His Patients.* New York: Crown, 1986.

Margery and Howard Facklam, *The Brain: Magnificent Mind Machine.* San Diego: Harcourt Brace Jovanovich, 1982.

Steve Fishman, *A Bomb in the Brain: A Heroic Tale of Science, Surgery and Survival.* New York: Avon Books, 1988.

Michael S. Gazzaniga, *Mind Matters: How Mind and Brain Interact to Create Our Conscious Lives*. Boston: Houghton Mifflin, 1988.

Jeff Goldberg, *Anatomy of a Scientific Discovery: The Race to Discover the Secret of Human Pain and Pleasure*. New York: Bantam Books, 1988.

Judith Hooper and Dick Teresi, *The Three-Pound Universe*. Los Angeles: Jeremy P. Tarcher, 1986.

How Things Work: The Brain. Alexandria, VA: Time-Life Books, 1990.

Darryl S. Inaba and William E. Cohen, *Uppers, Downers, All Arounders*. Ashland, OR: Cinemed, 1990.

Kenneth Klivington, *The Science of the Mind*. Cambridge, MA: MIT Press, 1989.

Jack Maguire and the Philip Leif Group, Inc., *Care and Feeding of the Brain: A Guide to Your Gray Matter*. New York: Doubleday, 1990.

Mind and Brain: Readings from Scientific American Magazine. New York: W. H. Freeman, 1993.

Anne Moir and David Jessel, *Brain Sex: The Real Difference Between Men and Women*. New York: Dell Books, 1993.

Anne D. Novitt-Moreno, *How Your Brain Works*. Emeryville, CA: Ziff-Davis, 1995.

Robert Ornstein and Richard F. Thompson, *The Amazing Brain*. Boston: Houghton Mifflin, 1984.

Richard M. Restak, *The Brain: The Last Frontier*. New York: Warner Books, 1979.

———, *The Brain Has a Mind of Its Own: Insights from a Practicing Neurologist*. New York: Harmony Books, 1991.

———, *The Mind*. New York: Bantam Books, 1988.

Oliver W. Sacks, *An Anthropologist on Mars: Seven Paradoxical Tales*. New York: Vintage Books, 1996.

Oliver W. Sacks, *The Man Who Mistook His Wife for a Hat: And Other Clinical Tales*. New York: HarperCollins, 1987.

Ron Van Der Meer, A.C.M. Dudink, and Pamela Clifford, *The Brain Pack: An Interactive, Three-Dimensional Exploration of the Mysteries of the Mind*. Philadelphia: Running Press, 1996.

ORGANIZATIONS

American Brain Tumor Association
2720 River Road, Suite 146
Des Plaines, IL 60018

Distributes "A Primer of Brain Tumors: A Patient's Reference Manual." E-mail ABTA@aol.com.

American Council for Headache Education
875 Kings Highway, Suite 200
Woodbury, NJ 08096

Free pamphlets include "What Can Be Done about Headache?" and "Why Does My Head Hurt?"

The American Parkinson's Disease Association
1250 Hylan Boulevard., Suite 4B
Staten Island, NY 10305

Request the pamphlet "Basic Information about Parkinson's Disease."

The Arc
National Headquarters
P.O. Box 1047
500 E. Border Street, S-300
Arlington, TX 76010

A national organization on mental retardation. Request a current list of publications.

Autism Society of America
7910 Woodmont Avenue, Suite 650
Bethesda, MD 20814-3015

Free pamphlet: "What Is Autism?"

Brain Injury Association, Inc.
1776 Massachusetts Avenue, NW
Suite 100
Washington, DC 20036-1904

Request a catalog of educational materials.

Epilepsy Foundation of America
4351 Garden City Drive
Landover, MD 20785-2267

Request the booklet "Questions and Answers about Epilepsy" or E-mail your inquiry to postmaster@efa.org.

Learning Disabilities Association
4156 Library Road
Pittsburgh, PA 15234

Fact sheet "When Learning Is a Problem." Website http://www.vcu.edu/eduweb/.

National Alliance for Research on Schizophrenia and Depression
60 Cutter Road, Suite 200
Great Neck, NY 11021

The Alliance distributes pamphlets and a free newsletter.

National Center for Learning Disabilities
381 Park Avenue South, Suite 1420
New York, NY 10016

Request most recent yearbook "Their World."

National Foundation for Depressive Illness, Inc.
P.O. Box 2257
New York, NY 10116

Distributes a newsletter, "NAFDI News."

National Institute of Mental Health
Public Inquiries, Room 7C-02
5600 Fishers Lane
Rockville, MD 20857

NIMH distributes a variety of useful pamphlets including "Bipolar Disorder" (95-3679) and "Panic Disorder" (95-3508). The Website for all National Institutes of Health is http://www.nih.gov.

National Mental Health Association
1021 Prince Street
Alexandria, VA 22314-2971

Free booklets include "How to Deal with Your Tensions" and "Depression: What You Should Know." Visit the Association's Website at http://www.worldcorp.com/dc-online/nmba.

The Orton Dyslexia Society
8600 LaSalle Road
Chester Building/ Suite 382
Baltimore, MD 21286-2044

Brochure is "Dyslexia: Defining the Problem." Visit Web page http://pie.org/ods or E-mail ods@pie.org.

Parkinson's Disease Foundation
Columbia-Presbyterian Medical Center
710 West 168 Street
New York, NY 10032

Request "Parkinson's Disease: Progress, Promise and Hope" or E-mail your inquiry to CPMC@aol.com.

Tourette Syndrome Association
42-40 Bell Boulevard
Bayside, NY 11361-2820

http://neuro-ww2.mgh.harvard.edu/TSA/tsamain.nclk.

GLOSSARY

Acetylcholine: See Table 2.

Alzheimer's disease: A degenerative disorder of thought, perception, and behavior most common among the elderly.

Amnesia: Difficulty learning new information or trouble remembering information or events from the past.

Amygdala: A part of the limbic system involved in forming memories.

Anoxia: Loss of oxygen supply to the brain.

Arteries: Blood vessels that carry blood (food and oxygen) to all organs of the body, including the heart and the brain.

Aspartate: See Table 2.

Auditory cortex: A portion of the temporal lobe that handles input from the ears (hearing).

Autism: A brain disorder characterized by self-absorption, repetitive movements, and an inability to relate socially.

Axon: A long projection from the cell body of a neuron. The axon of a motor neuron carries messages to muscles.

Blood-brain barrier: A network of tightly packed cells in the walls of capillaries in the brain that prevents many molecules—notably poisons—from passing into the brain.

Brain stem: The innermost base of the brain that controls automatic body functions such as breathing.

Broca's area: A speech center in the brain where thoughts are turned into speech.

Capillaries: Tiny blood vessels through which materials are exchanged between cells and the blood stream.

Cell body: The central mass of a neuron, containing the nucleus.

Cerebellum: A portion of the brain between the brain stem and the rear of the cerebrum that helps regulate posture, balance, and coordination.

Cerebrum: The "thinking" brain. See Cortex.

Classical conditioning: Training an animal (including a human) to respond to a stimulus with a reflex action.

Cones: Cells in the retina of the eyes that detect colors.

Corpus callosum: The bundle of fibers that connects the left and right hemispheres of the brain.

Cortex or cerebral cortex: The outermost layer of the cerebrum responsible for most of the brain's higher activities such as sensing, voluntary movement, language, conscious thought, and reasoning.

CT or computerized tomography: A process that uses X-rays and computers to take pictures of "slices" of the living brain.

Dendrites: Short projections from the cell bodies of neurons that receive signals from other neurons.

Depression: Severe persistent feelings of hopelessness, often accompanied by physical illness and suicidal thoughts.

Diffuse: To travel and mix gradually due to random movement of molecules.

Dopamine: See Table 2.

Dyslexia: A learning disability in which letters or numbers are jumbled.

ECT or electroconvulsive therapy: The induction of convulsions by applying electrical current to the brain; used in the treatment of severe depression.

EEG or electroencephalogram: A record of the electrical activity of the brain made by attaching electrodes to the scalp.

Endorphins: Endogenous morphines, or natural painkillers manufactured by the brain.

Engram: The hypothesized physical trace on the brain that might mark a memory. No engram has ever been found.

Enkephalin: A type of endorphin, the natural painkillers manufactured by the brain.

Epilepsy: A disorder of the brain in which random electrical discharges cause seizures.

Estrogen: A female hormone.

Excitatory receptor: A site on a neuron's membrane that, when bound by a neurotransmitter, makes a neuron more likely to fire. (If enough receptors are bound, it will fire.)

False memory syndrome: The "memory" of something that never happened.

Feedback: A process by which the result of a system's action controls its performance. An example is the thermostat of a furnace, which turns the furnace on when the air is cold and turns it off when the air is hot.

Frontal lobe: The lobe of the cerebral cortex under the forehead that controls planning, movement, and some aspects of speech.

Frontal lobotomy: An operation to cut the fiber linking the frontal lobes to other parts of the brain to control aggressive behavior, performed widely before 1960.

Functional MRI: A procedure that uses magnetic fields to take pictures of the brain at work.

GABA: See Table 2.

Glial cells: Cells that support neurons in the brain and create a chemical factor that strengthens communication between nerve cells. See Table 1.

Glutamate: See Table 2.

Hippocampus: A part of the brain (or limbic system) involved in forming memories.

Hormones: Chemicals made by one organ that travel through the bloodstream and affect another organ.

Hypnosis: A trancelike state in which a person becomes highly receptive to suggestion.

Hypothalamus: A part of the limbic system involved in regulating body functions and temperature, hunger, and thirst, and in secreting hormones that affect the body's "master gland," the pituitary.

Iconic memory: Photographic memory, which lasts for less than a tenth of a second.

Inhibitory receptor: A site on a neuron's membrane that, when bound by a neurotransmitter, makes a neuron less likely to fire. (If enough sites are bound, firing is blocked.)

Instinct: A behavior that is inborn; that is, it need not be learned.

Interneuron: A nerve cell that carries a message between a sensory neuron and a motor neuron.

Ion: A charged atom or molecule.

Ion pump or sodium-potassium pump: A mechanism in the membrane of a nerve cell that pumps sodium out of the axon (and potassium back in) after a signal has passed.

Isotopes: Atoms of an element that differ in their number of neutrons.

Limbic system: A group of structures in the brain including the hypothalamus, hippocampus, and amygdala known to help control basic body functions as well as emotion, motivation, and memory.

Locus coeruleus: An area in the brain stem that can wake the nondreaming sleeper. Also involved in feeding behavior.

Long-term memory: Permanent memory of information, events, or skills.

LTP or long-term potentiation: The conditioning of neurons to respond again as they have before. Thought to be the cellular basis of learning.

Membrane: A thin outer covering, such as that surrounding a cell.

Meninges: The three membranes that surround and protect the brain and spinal cord.

Mitochondria: The structures in cells where energy is released from food.

Motor neuron: A nerve cell that carries a signal from the brain (or spinal cord) to a muscle, causing it to contract.

MRI or magnetic resonance imaging: A procedure that uses magnetic fields to take pictures of the structure of the brain.

Myelin: An insulating material produced by glial cells that wraps around axons.

Nerves: Bundles of axons and dendrites that carry messages back and forth between parts of the body and the spinal cord and brain.

Neuron: Nerve cell. See Table 1.

Neurotransmitter: A chemical released from the axon of a nerve cell that crosses the synapse to the dendrite of the next neuron, causing it to fire and thereby transmit a message. Neurotransmitters bind to receptor sites much as keys fit into locks.

Neurotrophic factors: See Table 2.

Norepinephrine: See Table 2.

Nucleus: The dense central mass in a cell that acts as its control center. Can also mean a collection of cell bodies within the brain such as the caudate nucleus.

Occipital lobe: The lobe of the cerebral cortex at the back of the head that includes the visual cortex.

Operant conditioning: A method for training behavior using reward or punishment.

Opioids: See Endorphins, Enkephalin, and Table 2.

Parietal lobe: The lobe of the cerebral cortex at the crown of the head that receives and processes data from the senses.

Parkinson's disease: A movement disorder most common among the elderly.

Peptides: Short chains of amino acids.

PET or positron emission tomography: A procedure that uses radioactive isotopes to create images of the brain at work.

Phrenology. The erroneous idea that bumps on the skull reveal personality.

Pituitary gland: A gland that secretes many hormones that affect other organs and systems, including blood pressure, growth, reproduction and sexual behavior, and blood-sugar levels.

Placebo effect: The observed tendency among some individuals to be relieved of disease symptoms by belief in a drug or treatment known to have no actual therapeutic benefit.

Primary memory: Short-term memory, which lasts for about 15-20 seconds.

Pruning: The loss of unused connections between neurons.

Psychosurgery: Brain surgery to alleviate seizures or alter behavior.

Receptor: A site on the surface of a cell membrane that binds a particular molecule, much as a lock accepts a key.

REM sleep: A period of rapid eye movements during sleep.

Resting potential: The difference in electrical charge between the inside and the outside of a nerve cell when the cell is not firing.

Reticular formation: A network of neurons in the brain stem involved in sleeping and waking.

Retrograde messenger: A chemical or process that can strengthen the bond between neurons; a possible mechanism for long-term potentiation. See LTP.

Rods: Cells in the retina of the eye that work best in dim light and detect shades of gray.

Schizophrenia: A disease of the brain characterized by disordered thoughts, false beliefs, and abnormal behaviors.

Secondary memory: Working memory that allows retention of information and processes long enough to work through a problem, situation, or experience.

Sensory neuron: A nerve cell that carries impulses from the sense organs to the brain or spinal cord.

Serotonin: See Table 2.

Short-term memory: See Primary memory.

Spatial reasoning: The brain's ability to form mental pictures of objects and move them around in imaginary space.

Spinal cord: Bundles of neurons encased by the backbone. The cord carries messages between the brain and the rest of the body.

Synapse: The axon of one neuron, the dendrite of another, adjacent neuron and the gap between them.

Temporal lobe: The lobe of the cerebral cortex at the side of the head that hears and interprets music and language.

Thalamus: A part of the brain just above the hypothalamus responsible for relaying sensory information to the cortex.

Ventricles: Fluid-filled cavities in the brain.

Visual cortex: A portion of the occipital lobe that handles data from the eyes.

Wavelength: The distance between the peaks (or the valleys) of a lightwave.

Wernicke's area: A center in the brain responsible for understanding speech.

Working memory: See Secondary memory.

INDEX